SOUTHERN LITERARY STUDIES

Fred Hobson, *Editor*

AUTOBIOGRAPHY IN WALKER PERCY

AUTOBIOGRAPHY
IN
WALKER
PERCY

Repetition, Recovery, and Redemption

Edward J. Dupuy

LOUISIANA STATE UNIVERSITY PRESS

Baton Rouge and London

Designer: Rebecca Lloyd Lemna
Typeface: Galliard
Typesetter: Impressions, a division of Edwards Brothers, Inc.
Printer and binder: Thomson-Shore, Inc.

The author is grateful to Mrs. Mary Bernice Townsend Percy, Shelby Foote, and the Southern Historical Collection, Library of the University of North Carolina at Chapel Hill, for permission to quote from unpublished materials in the Walker Percy Papers, #4294, and the Shelby Foote Papers, #4038.

Part of Chapter 1 was first published, in somewhat different form, as "Being Interested in Time: Autobiography and Repetition," *Listening,* XXVIII (Spring, 1993), 141–57, and is reprinted with permission.

Library of Congress Cataloging-in-Publication Data
Dupuy, Edward J., 1958–
    Autobiography in Walker Percy : repetition, recovery, and
redmeption / Edward J. Dupuy.
        p.   cm. — (Southern literary studies)
    Includes bibliographical references (p.   ) and index.
    ISBN 0-8071-2012-X (cloth : alk. paper)
    1. Percy, Walker, 1916– —Criticism and interpretation.
2. Autobiographical fiction, American—History and criticism.
3. Southern States—In literature. 4. Repetition in literature.
5. Redemption in literature. 6. Self in literature.
7. Autobiography. I. Title. II. Series.
PS3566.E6912Z66   1996
813'.54—dc20   95-23388
                                                                    CIP

For Polly and John

Contents

Preface

If it is true that critics are closet autobiographers, that whatever they write about someone else's work inevitably bears the impression of their own lives and selves, then readers should be forewarned; you are undertaking an exploration into my life.

I first became aware of Walker Percy sometime during my student years at Saint Joseph Seminary College, a small liberal arts college in Covington, Louisiana. This is the same school where Percy taught one year and where he delivered the commencement address in 1983, later reprinted in *Signposts in a Strange Land* as "A Cranky Novelist Reflects on the Church." He was an acquaintance of the president-rector of the college—a "priest-sociologist"—and I saw them from time to time walking around the campus. I was not an avid reader during those years, so when I learned that Percy wrote novels, I did not rush out to get one of his books. I did have occasion, however, to buy *Love in the Ruins* for a friend during the summer of 1979. I bought it at the Kumquat, the bookstore in Covington owned by Percy's daughter, Anne Moores. Mrs. Mary Bernice Townsend Percy happened to be working in the store when I went in. After I paid for the book, she said, "Walker is working upstairs. He'll be down in a few minutes if you'd like to talk to him." Being somewhat like Will Barrett of *The Last Gentleman,* an affable albeit "addled young man," I declined. What was I going to say to this man? Why should I want to talk to him? So I took the book, wrote a note to my friend, a large part of which I copied from the dust cover—something about the "apocalyptic" nature of the work—and delivered it. Later on, I bought a paperback copy for myself, read it, and became even more addled. I enjoyed the story, what I could make of it, enjoyed the descriptions of the "Love Clinic" and Tom More's lapsometer, but I had no idea what Percy was up to. All the same, I sensed that he was "onto something." So I read it again. Soon, I was hooked. I had to read his other books.

I gradually realized that this man was writing about me. It was not an altogether pleasant realization, for if you know Percy's characters, you know that they are a rather wounded lot. How could he know me so well? How could he show me my own wounds?

Some fourteen years later, I seek in this study an answer to those questions. I return, then, to the place I began. I think it is accurate for me to say that in reading Walker Percy I gained my introduction to the world of letters. I would like this study to be seen as a tribute to him whose work has opened new possibilities for me. I can only hope that it is a fitting tribute.

Along the way, of course, I've had lots of help. If the book has anything inviting and enduring about it—two qualities that both fiction and criticism strive for—it is partly because of those from whom I have received so much.

Thus, I wish to thank my parents for their abundant generosity. To my wife, Jan, I say thanks for everything, but especially for the time and support I needed to get this work done. To our three children—Benjamin, Madeleine, and John—I say thanks for enduring a sometimes grumpy dad and a closed study door.

I would also like to thank several people at Louisiana State University: James Olney, whose wisdom and encouragement offered themselves as quiet guides; and John R. May, whose keen eye challenged me to sharpen my prose. Thanks, too, to Peggy Whitman Prenshaw, John Lowe, John Whittaker, and David H. Smyth. Professor Lewis P. Simpson, ever generous of time, insight, and spirit, offered his valuable comments and encouragement during early versions of the manuscript and beyond, as did Patrick Samway, S.J., and Fred Hobson. Sr. Jeanne d'Arc Kernion, O.S.B., and Mrs. Jennie Vincent LeBeau kindly proofread the typescript for me.

Mrs. Mary Bernice Townsend Percy was very generous with materials such as audio- and videotapes that came from her private collection. I am grateful for those, and for the copy of Henry Kisor's memoir that she provided. I want to thank her, too, for permission to quote from her late husband's letters and papers. Shelby Foote was equally generous in allowing me to use his letters to Dr. Percy.

The monks of Saint Joseph Abbey and Seminary College not only gave me a foundation in the liberal arts several years ago but also furnished me with a study away from home. Special thanks are due Fr. Matthew Clark, O.S.B., who provided me the use of a computer, and to Fr. Adrian Hovey, O.S.B., who helped set it up. With regard to computers, I want to thank also René B. deLaup, whose wizardry and expertise saved me countless hours of work, and Marc Fluitt.

I also want to extend a general thanks to the interlibrary loan staff at Middleton Library at LSU and to the staff of the Southern Historical Collection, Library of the University of North Carolina, Chapel Hill. Among the works I consulted while writing this book, Linda Whitney Hobson's *Walker Percy: A Comprehensive Descriptive Bibliography* (New Orleans, 1988) was especially useful to me.

Finally, thanks are due the staff at LSU Press, especially John Easterly, who maintained a gentle demeanor even while barraged with my anxious letters and questions. Thanks, too, to Nicola Mason, who walked me through the tedious process of copyediting.

Abbreviations

Except for *The Moviegoer,* which was published by Alfred A. Knopf, all of Percy's books cited here were published by Farrar, Straus and Giroux.

Con	*Conversations with Walker Percy.* Jackson, 1985
L	*Lancelot.* 1977
LC	*Lost in the Cosmos.* 1983
LG	*The Last Gentleman.* 1966
LR	*Love in the Ruins.* 1971
MB	*The Message in the Bottle.* 1975
MCon	*More Conversations with Walker Percy.* Jackson, 1993
MG	*The Moviegoer.* 1961
SC	*The Second Coming.* 1980
SHC	Southern Historical Collection, Library of the University of North Carolina, Chapel Hill. Letters and Papers.
Signposts	*Signposts in a Strange Land.* 1991
TS	*The Thanatos Syndrome.* 1987

AUTOBIOGRAPHY IN WALKER PERCY

Introduction

We shall not cease

from exploration

And the end of

all our exploring

Will be to arrive

where we started

And know the place

for the first time.

—T. S. Eliot,

"Little Gidding"

The search is what

anyone would undertake

if he were not sunk in

the everydayness of

his own life.

—Binx Bolling,

The Moviegoer

During an interview in 1981, J. Gerald Kennedy asked Walker Percy, "When your biography is written, are we going to see your novels in those terms?" Percy replied candidly: "Oh, I guess some of it, but not in the current sense of a roman à clef. Not because I think there is anything wrong with it, but I mean the American vogue of writing a roman à clef to me is a big bore. It's no fun. The fun comes in transforming experience, taking something that's happened to you, something you might imagine that happened—or I'm talking to you and I could imagine something that might have happened to you—and putting the pieces all together; that's where the fun is" (*Con*, 239).

At first glance Percy's comment does not seem altogether significant. For what he admits must undoubtedly transpire in almost every writer. Writers transform experience—lived or imagined—into art.[1] But what does it mean to transform experience? Transform

---

1. The first biography of Percy has now been written, and in *Pilgrim in the Ruins: A Life of Walker Percy* (New York, 1992), Jay Tolson shows clearly the transformations Percy makes from his life to his fiction.

comes from the Latin prefix *trans*, "across, implying change," and *formare*, "to form." Experience has its roots in *experientia*, which means "a trial or a test." To transform experience, then, would be "to change across the form of a trial," or better, "to change the form of a trial."[2]

Although Percy uses *experience* in this interview to signify the more or less "ordinary" understanding of the word, that is, "an actual living through an event or events," his comment gains significance when placed in the context of the existentialist philosophy that he found so illuminating. For, as he states time and again in his essays and novels, experience, the actual living through events, has returned to its original sense and has itself become a trial: "How does one live through an ordinary Wednesday afternoon?" This ostensibly innocent question provides much of the impetus for Percy's writing.

Following his existentialist progenitors, Percy wonders whether one actually "lives" through events anymore. It seems, on the contrary, that a pervasive sense of death prevails. The "gas of malaise," "ravening particles," and "death-in-life" becloud and bombard attempts at ordinary living and pit his characters against the seductions of death. As Binx Bolling reflects in *The Moviegoer*, "for some time now the impression has been growing on me that everyone is dead" (99). And the older Will Barrett asks in *The Second Coming*, "Am I killed and until this moment did not know it?" (147). Or again, "Is it possible for people to miss their lives in the same way one misses a plane?" (124). Percy's last novel even has death in its title: *The Thanatos Syndrome*. He speaks for himself (and more directly) in his essay "Notes for a Novel About the End of the World": "The hero of the postmodern novel is a man who has forgotten his bad memories and conquered his present ills and who finds himself in the victorious secular city. His only problem now is to keep from blowing his brains out" (*MB*, 112).

While Percy's heroes have not necessarily forgotten their "bad memories"—Binx ponders his father's death; Will Barrett confronts his father's suicide both in *The Last Gentleman* and, more powerfully, in *The Second Coming*; Tom More remembers his daughter's ugly death; and *Lancelot* is built on the recovering memory of Lancelot Lamar—they nevertheless

2. Etymologies taken from *Webster's New Universal Unabridged Dictionary* (New York, 1979).

struggle constantly with what might be called the "postmodern" task of "living" through ordinary experience. The "old modern age," as Tom More sees it, has passed. How is one to live now, in the postmodern era?

As Percy's response to Kennedy's question suggests, Percy often found experience a trial, and the "fun" of writing his novels came about in changing the form of that trial. In a general sense this transformation, of course, is the autobiographical movement. Commenting on what by now must be considered the classic work in the field of autobiography, *Metaphors of Self: The Meaning of Autobiography,* James Olney writes about his own work:

> When I began (in about 1966) to write what eventually became *Metaphors of Self* it never occurred to me to look for critical works on autobiography for the simple reason that I did not think of what I was doing as a study of autobiography; I thought of it as a study of the way *experience is transformed into literature* (which I suppose could be another way of describing autobiography)—as a study of the creative process, a humanistic study of the ways of men and the forms taken by human consciousness.[3]

The uncanny similarity between Percy's comment and the words I have italicized in Olney's passage opens the door not only to an understanding of Percy's works in an autobiographical context but also (and more importantly) to an appreciation of autobiography in light of Percy's own studies of "the ways of men and the forms taken by human consciousness."

Of course, readers familiar with the extensive criticism that Percy's writing has generated know that that metaphorical door has already been opened. Jay Tolson's *Pilgrim in the Ruins,* William Rodney Allen's *Walker Percy: A Southern Wayfarer,* and Bertram Wyatt-Brown's *The House of Percy* all trace such transformations of experience into art—Tolson, particularly, Allen, more generally, and Wyatt-Brown, historically. Allen's emphasis on the role of "fathers"—literal, adoptive, and literary—places Percy's fiction in an explicit autobiographical context, for Allen argues convincingly that "Percy's fiction is in a very real sense his response to his father's suicide." Tolson, on the other hand, suggests that the "absent mother" plays a central

---

3. James Olney, *Metaphors of Self: The Meaning of Autobiography* (Princeton, 1972); James Olney, "Autobiography and the Cultural Moment: A Thematic, Historical, and Bibliographical Introduction," in *Autobiography: Essays Theoretical and Critical,* ed. James Olney (Princeton, 1980), 10.

role in defining Percy's works: "Where . . . are the mothers among all those chaotically brooding father figures who dominate the memories of Percy's fictional heroes?" Wyatt-Brown, for his part, argues that Percy's novels exhibit "many of the family's innermost values."[4]

While these writers unlock the mysteries of Percy's fiction with the keys of his personal experience, I explore the "fun" of transforming experience at a more general level. I look at Percy's works (fiction and nonfiction) to discern their relation to the *autos, bios,* and *graphein* of autobiography. Thus, I do not examine so much the correspondences between Percy's life and work. Nor do I merely "apply" autobiographical theory in an umbrella-like fashion to his works. What interests me, rather, is Percy's continual and repetitive "picking of the bone" of the same issues theorists of autobiography pick. Percy's questions regarding self and life (and their relation to language and writing) disclose the germs not only of his hoped-for "theory of man" but also of an autobiographical theory. My study, then, sets forth not so much an "autobiographical reading" of Percy's works but a reading of autobiography in light of his works. The two, of course, are connected. I call upon autobiographical theory to disclose parallels to Percy's works, and Percy's works, in turn, to disclose new vistas of autobiographical theory.

It becomes apparent, furthermore, that Percy's continual picking of this bone places repetition at the center of his life and writing. His readings of Kierkegaard, who views repetition as a movement in which "everything is returned double,"[5] and Heidegger, who refines Kierkegaard's notion to include a "retrieval" of foreclosed possibilities, brought Percy to an understanding of repetition as both an "importunate" bonus and a retrieval. Both Kierkegaard and Heidegger agonize over the placement of the self in time, and so does Percy. In Percy's works, then, repetition comes to be understood as an effort to redeem time, to make it once again inhabitable. It is, in the end, an effort to establish a place for the self that is between (*inter esse*) the polarities of experience that would divorce it from time. Percy's

4. William Rodney Allen, *Walker Percy: A Southern Wayfarer* (Jackson, 1986), xvii; Tolson, *Pilgrim,* 142; Bertram Wyatt-Brown, *The House of Percy: Honor, Melancholy, and Imagination in a Southern Family* (New York, 1994), 20.

5. Søren Kierkegaard, *Fear and Trembling/Repetition,* ed. and trans. Howard V. Hong and Edna H. Hong (Princeton, 1983), 220.

works reveal the self in a struggle to retrieve its proper inheritance and thus to become engaged once again in time. *Inter esse,* as William V. Spanos has shown, encompasses both being and time in its dual meaning: "being between" and "concerned."[6] Percy's works and autobiography both lead to the same end—the desire of a self to locate itself in time. That is to say, there is a sense in which autobiographers recover, regain, or, as we shall see, "repeat" their experience (as do Percy's characters) so that they are able once again to live in that experience. They thus attain a type of reconciliation and redemption.

It is interesting and entirely germane to my argument that autobiography is a relatively recent entrant in the many fields of critical inquiry. Almost every critic of autobiography with whom I am familiar has commented on this fact.[7] Yet it is Olney who offers lucid insights as to why this might be. According to Olney autobiography has found its place in this cultural moment for three reasons, the first related to genre and the second two to criticism: "First, there is the dual, paradoxical fact that autobiography is often something considerably less than literature and that it is always something rather more than literature. . . . It refuses, simply, to be a literary genre like any other." James Cox seems to say something similar when he writes that autobiography as a genre exists somewhere between the self-enclosed and self-referential literature of imagination and the purely referential literature of fact.[8] Autobiography, then, defies any facile generic classification.

Olney continues: "A second, related reason . . . is that critics of twenty-

6. William V. Spanos, *Repetitions: The Postmodern Occasion in Literature and Culture* (Baton Rouge, 1987), 99.

7. See Olney, "Cultural Moment," in *Autobiography: Essays,* ed. Olney; see also Robert F. Sayre, "Autobiography and the Making of America," in *Autobiography: Essays,* ed. Olney, 146; Janet Varner Gunn, *Autobiography: Toward a Poetics of Experience* (Philadelphia, 1982), 3; Paul John Eakin, *Fictions in Autobiography: Studies in the Art of Self-Invention* (Princeton, 1985); James M. Cox, *Recovering Literature's Lost Ground: Essays in American Autobiography* (Baton Rouge, 1989).

8. Olney, "Cultural Moment," in *Autobiography: Essays,* ed. Olney, 24, 25; Cox, *Recovering Literature's Lost Ground,* 8.

five years ago insisted that for satisfying aesthetic apprehension a work must display (in Stephen Dedalus' phrase) 'wholeness, harmony, and radiance.' " While some autobiographers may strive for the latter two of Dedalus' triad, the first, in the sense of a completed and closed work is for autobiography an impossibility: "The end of the story cannot be told. . . . The narrative is never finished, nor ever can be, within the covers of a book."[9]

Here Olney implicitly refers to the shift that has occurred in literary studies during the last few decades. That is, he refers to the change in allegiance from the New Critical (modernist) paradigm—a model that, as William V. Spanos and others have shown, takes its credo directly from Joyce's *A Portrait of the Artist as a Young Man* and that holds "timelessness" in priority to time—to the deconstructive or destructive (postmodern) criticism that has its origins in existential philosophy and that places an emphasis on time, a model that itself has been supplanted in recent years.[10] I will treat this shift in perspective in more detail in Chapter 1—especially the relation between autobiography and time, for as Olney says in another context, the autobiographer's prime motive is to "redeem the time." But it is enough to say now that autobiography, based on these first two reasons alone, can be viewed as a prime postmodern form, inasmuch as postmodernism has a form.

The third reason for autobiography's delayed entry into the circles of critical inquiry has to do with its self-reflexive nature (in spite of Cox's above claim, or maybe in addition to it, since he places autobiography in

9. Olney, "Cultural Moment," in *Autobiography: Essays,* ed. Olney, 25.

10. Spanos, *Repetitions,* articles: "The Indifference of *Différance:* Retrieving Heidegger's De-struction," *Annals of Scholarship,* II (1981), 109–29; "Heidegger, Kierkegaard, and the Hermeneutic Circle: Toward a Postmodern Theory of Interpretation as Disclosure," *boundary 2,* IV (1976), 455–88; "Modern Drama and the Aristotelian Tradition: The Formal Imperatives of Absurd Time," *Contemporary Literature,* XII (1971), 345–73; "Modern Literary Criticism and the Spatialization of Time," *Journal of Aesthetics and Art Criticism,* XXIX (1970), 87–104; " 'Wanna Go Home, Baby?': *Sweeney Agonistes* as Drama of the Absurd," *PMLA,* LXXXV (1968), 8–20; "The Critical Imperatives of Alienation: The Theological Perspective of Nathan Scott's Literary Criticism," *Journal of Religion,* XLVIII (1968), 89–103. See also Paul A. Bové, "Cleanth Brooks and Modern Irony: A Kierkegaardian Critique," *boundary 2,* IV (1976), 727–59; Nathan A. Scott, Jr., *The Broken Center: Studies in the Theological Horizon of Modern Literature* (New Haven, 1966); Joseph Frank, "Spatial Form in Modern Literature," *Sewanee Review,* LIII (1945), 221–40, 432–56, 643–53.

the middle, which would mean, of course, that it is self-reflexive to a degree). As Olney phrases it, "autobiography is a self-reflexive, a self-critical act, and consequently the criticism of autobiography exists *within* the literature instead of alongside it. The autobiographer can discuss and analyze the autobiographical act as he performs it."[11] From St. Augustine's reflections on time and memory in his *Confessions* to Mary McCarthy's italicized, complementary sections in *Memories of a Catholic Girlhood* to Ronald Fraser's fascinating blend of subjective and objective history (psychoanalysis and interviews) in his *In Search of a Past,* autobiographers theorize about their work even as they enact it.[12]

Percy, of course, never wrote what is commonly considered an autobiography. He once wrote Tolson: "The only thing more boring than writing my own memoir is the prospect of collaborating with somebody on a biography." Instead, his forms of choice were the essay and the novel. While he never completely abandoned the essay form, I agree with Patricia Lewis Poteat, who maintains that it is the novel that is best suited to Percy's aims as a writer. She argues that "Percy's conceptual vision becomes progressively more blurred as his style and vocabulary become progressively less anecdotal or narrative and more analytical and abstract—hence, ever more tenuously anchored in the concrete particulars of persons in predicaments."[13] Those essays that incorporate anecdote and narrative (persons in predicaments)—essays that might be called "novelistic," such as "The Man on the Train," "The Loss of the Creature," and "The Message in the Bottle"—she claims, are clearer and more persuasive than the technical and more abstract essays in *The Message in the Bottle*. While I agree with Poteat's basic claim, I think that what she "discovers" about Percy's behavioral stance in the essays is off the mark. On the one hand, she does not consider the rhetorical situation of each essay—*i.e.,* its audience—as does Robert Coles, for example.[14] On the other hand, she seems to disallow any incon-

11. James Olney, "Some Versions of Memory/Some Versions of *Bios:* The Ontology of Autobiography," in *Autobiography: Essays,* ed. Olney, 240, Olney's emphasis.

12. Saint Augustine, *The Confessions of St. Augustine,* trans. Rex Warner (New York, 1963); Mary McCarthy, *Memories of a Catholic Girlhood* (New York, 1957); Ronald Fraser, *In Search of a Past: The Manor House, Amnersfield, 1933–1945* (London, 1984).

13. Tolson, *Pilgrim,* 9; Patricia Louis Poteat, *Walker Percy and the Old Modern Age: Reflections on Language, Argument and the Telling of Stories* (Baton Rouge, 1985), 2.

14. Robert Coles, *Walker Percy: An American Search* (Boston, 1978), 53–117.

gruity in Percy's thought. He was, after all, trying to bridge a gap, as he says, between theorizing about "man" and theorizing about animals: "So you have this tremendous gap between accounting for animals and their behavior, which can be done by fairly adequate mechanistic models, and accounting for man, who can erect theories and utter sentences about these very creatures" (*Con,* 134). It is surprising, too, that Poteat makes little reference to the essays collected in *Signposts;* although uncollected at the time of her writing, most of them were nevertheless available in their original form. Nor does she refer to the Intermezzo section of *Lost in the Cosmos,* a work Percy once called his most important achievement (*Con,* 285). Percy himself, however, was aware of the problem Poteat suggests with regard to his essays: tired of "getting paid in reprints," interested in the novels of Jean-Paul Sartre and Albert Camus, writers who "see nothing wrong with writing novels that address what they consider the deepest philosophical issues," and eager to reach a broader audience than his essays allowed, Percy turned to novel writing during the 1950s.[15]

His first two efforts—"The Charterhouse" and "The Gramercy Winner"—were, by his own admission, terrible: "[I wrote] two bad novels which I'm glad were not published."[16] He made his breakthrough with *The Moviegoer,* published in 1961 and the winner of the 1962 National Book Award. The rest, as the saying goes, is history. His writing career spanned the next thirty years of his life: *The Last Gentleman* (1966), *Love in the Ruins* (1971), *The Message in the Bottle* (1975), *Lancelot* (1977), *The Second Coming* (1980), *Lost in the Cosmos* (1983), *The Thanatos Syndrome* (1987), and *Signposts in a Strange Land* (1991), the posthumously published collection of essays, edited by Patrick Samway, S.J., the second of Percy's biographers.[17]

But this foray into chronology steers me away from my principal concern with Percy's novels and his view of the novel. For Percy's view of the novel and the characteristics of autobiography outlined above share much and thus further signal the aptness of an autobiographical approach to his works. Percy's comments in essays and interviews about the novel being a

15. *Con,* 183; Coles, *Walker Percy,* 137.

16. *Con,* 89; "The Gramercy Winner" is available at the Southern Historical Collection at UNC–Chapel Hill.

17. Samway's biography is still "in-progress" at the time of this writing.

"mess" or having been "always in trouble," for example, correspond not only to the "oppositional poetics" Walter Reed discusses in *An Exemplary History of the Novel,* but also to the generic instability that Olney sees in autobiography. Furthermore, Percy's view of the novel as "diagnostic" and ultimately therapeutic, what Michael McKeon calls its "problem-solving mode," seems to correspond to the autobiographer's attempt to name himself by writing his life.[18] Although naming a problem is the first step to solving it, giving a name entails a fall of sorts, a misname, for Percy. And since the self, as I will show in Chapter 2, is semiotically adrift, and since, as Percy writes in "Metaphor as Mistake," we can only know "one thing through the lens of another" (*MB,* 82), it is precisely through the attempt to name that a subject opens itself to the possibility of being a self. Of course, this striving after a name presupposes that the self is problematical in the first place; otherwise, why try to name it? The self cannot be so readily named as other things because it is not a thing among other things, but a nothing. Thus, and this relates Percy's novel writing to autobiography all the more firmly, the attempt to name is lifelong and hence without closure.

Furthermore, Percy sees the novel as an excellent medium for depicting what Marcel called *homo viator,* man the wayfarer or pilgrim (*Con,* 231). Such a wayfarer, however, cannot reach his end. For if the novel is about "man on the road," then the road, quite literally, can have no terminus. Some critics have chided Percy for his ambiguous endings (except for *The Second Coming,* which was criticized for its apparent closure!), but it is precisely that ambiguity that points to the openness of possibility and the lifelong process of self-naming. Both autobiography and Percy's novels, then, struggle with the question of time, whose end remains unknown, but which nevertheless seems to demand redemption. That is to say, both Percy's writing and autobiography share a goal of calling the writer (and the reader) back to an awareness of time, of the self's placement in time, through the process of self-naming.

The correspondence between the self-reflexive nature of autobiography and Percy's work is less clear. Instead of making his novels self-reflexive, as Faulkner does, for example, in *Absalom, Absalom!,* Percy seems to have used

18. Walter Reed, *An Exemplary History of the Novel* (Chicago, 1981), 3–4; Michael McKeon, *The Origins of the English Novel, 1600–1740* (Baltimore, 1987), 21.

the essay and the interview to reflect on the nature of writing. Nevertheless, as I have noted, his works taken as a whole suggest a theory of autobiography. Furthermore, his narrative style displays an interpenetration of form and content, if you will. Repetition is both a theme in Percy's works and an element of his writing style. In this sense his works can be read as exhibiting a self-reflexivity.

This study, then, strives to introduce several new approaches to Percy's works. It looks, not so much for a one-to-one relation between Percy's life and his works, but for the broader relations between autobiography, repetition, and language in the works as a whole. Percy's "bone to pick" in his writings on language lead him to and from his fictional creations. Thus there is a sense in which he looks both backward and forward: backward over his life and the dislocation he experienced in time and space; forward toward the hope, first, that his pilgrimage might be made meaningful in language and time, and ultimately toward that hope he gained from his commitment to Roman Catholicism. As Percy reflects on language he also seeks to create a new language in which his message (and he himself) might be conveyed.

To say that Percy's works are autobiographical, then, does not mean that they point inexorably and solely to their creator. It does not mean that Percy has joined the ranks of the solipsistic culture he so deftly critiqued. It means rather that Percy, like the autobiographer and like theorists of autobiography, engages in questions of the self in relation to language and consciousness and time. What emerges from those reflections is the radical "betweenness" (*inter esse*) of repetition. Between angel and beast, world and environment, consumer and scientist, immanence and transcendence, the self Percy explores leads him (and the reader) outward to the mystery of the self in time and consciousness and language. In a culture in which language has been devalued, where "words no longer signify," naming has no meaning. The modernists often worried about the slippage between the signifier and the signified, and the postmodernists revel in their rupture, but Percy acknowledges something of both. He argues, like the modernists, that a sign signifies; it means, or it should mean, something definite. Yet, like the postmodernists, he argues that a gap between the signifier and the signified is necessary in order for meaning to reveal itself. On the one hand, the attempt to close or harden the gap between the two results in a dead language, and the self likewise collapses on itself. On the other hand, a too cavalier disjunction between the two produces a vacuous language, and the self becomes rarefied. Percy wants it both ways. He wants the density of meaning and the space for the disclosure of meaning. He wants a self that displays itself as *inter esse,* being between and concerned in time. A right understanding of language, Percy suggests, retrieves the rightful inheritance of the language user.

The autobiographer and the novelist both seek a place for the self in language. Yet a culture that seems unconcerned with the loss of the value of language falls prey to the abstractions of Gnosticism. Life in time becomes a trial from which the only possible escape of the self from itself is death. The Gnostic seeks to destroy time in order to liberate his "true self," but the autobiographer and the novelist seek to redeem time so that the self might again find reason for hope. It is no wonder, then, that a strong anti-Gnostic stance pervades Percy's works. Percy seeks to retrieve and reestablish the self in language and time, even as that self is unaware of its Gnostic predicament. For the autobiographer, and for Percy as autobiographer, language provides the starting point for an exploration of such a possibility. Language repeats, retrieves, and transforms experience into art while at the same time it points toward future possibilities.

This study strives for much the same thing. While the chapters can be read autonomously, each nevertheless foreshadows the next and builds upon the previous one. Thus, this study of repetition evinces a degree of repetition. Chapter 1 explores the connections between autobiography and time and tries to relate such an understanding of autobiography to Percy's understanding of the novel as diagnostic. I make explicit here the theoretical underpinnings on which the rest of the book depends. Chapters 2, 3, and 4 explore different aspects of repetition and autobiography, specifically with regard to the roots of the word: self, life, and writing. Chapter 2 examines Percy's contention that the self is unformulable in language and thus a *homo viator.* Chapter 3 probes the consequences of life in a century of Gnosticism and death, with specific reference to Percy's implicit treatment of the Nazi genocide of the Jews. Chapter 4 explores the interrelation between repetition as a theme and as a narrative technique. Finally, a coda "repeats" many of the themes developed in the work but reflects more on Percy the man. Just as self, life, and writing coalesce in the word *autobiography,* so are they repeated in the works of Walker Percy.

1

Autobiography, Repetition, and Percy

When the novelist writes of a man "coming to himself" through some such catalyst as catastrophe or ordeal, he may be offering obscure testimony to a gross disorder of consciousness and to the need of recovering oneself as neither angel nor organism but as a wayfaring creature somewhere between.

—Walker Percy,
"Notes for a Novel About
the End of the World"

And what petty precision to quibble about locations in space or in chronology.

—William Faulkner,
"Raid"

One of the problems any writer confronts in developing an autobiographical study is the setting of limits to the term. That is to say, how does one define *autobiography*? Is there such a thing as a genre called autobiography that is characteristically different from other genres? What are the boundaries that set it off from other types of writing?

The *OED* defines autobiography as "the writing of one's own history; the story of one's life written by himself."[1] This seems to be a fair assessment of the term; yet what can be considered as one's "history"? Is it a simple compilation of the events that occur during the course of one's lifetime? And if so, how does one pattern those events, or can there be a pattern at all? Is it true that a pattern distorts, in some way, the material it comprises? Or is it more truthful to say that when one writes something in narrative form, a pattern is established or assumed in the very act of writing itself, and that writing without

1. This definition is taken from the 1971 edition of the *OED*.

13

a pattern carries no significance beyond individual words? Furthermore, how can one account for those autobiographies, such as Herbert Read's *The Innocent Eye,* that contain very little reference to actual events? In short, this definition begs the question of history and historiography.

Nor do the waters become less murky when one turns to a definition of *story*. Cannot poetry be considered, in some sense, the story of its writer? And if so, why not a collection of essays, a philosophy, a theology, or a series of novels? If a story implies a pattern, as the *OED* suggests, then practically any narrative could be considered autobiography. The genre, if indeed I can even use that word, cannot be so readily cataloged.

But none of this is new to the study of autobiography. I have cited Olney and Cox, who say that autobiography is both more and less than literature. In *Metaphors of Self,* Olney explicitly eschews any generic approach to the field: "It is not at all my present purpose to try to define a literary form, or to distinguish and classify all the varieties and types of autobiography; indeed, definition of autobiography as a literary genre seems to me virtually impossible, because the definition must either include so much as to be no definition, or exclude so much as to deprive us of the most relevant texts. Either way, definition is not particularly desirable or significant."[2]

But if Olney denies any explicit definition of autobiography, his theory—the preceding quotation is taken from his chapter entitled "A Theory of Autobiography"—suggests an implicit one. Autobiography creates a metaphor of self for both its writer and its reader. It names the self through the process of metaphorical indirection. Autobiography is that type of writing that creates and names a metaphor of self. Granted, this "definition" leaves much to be clarified—something Olney does throughout the remainder of his book in his discussions of Eliot, Jung, Montaigne, and others; nevertheless, it is a definition of sorts.

Theorists of autobiography seem to escape the trap of definition through an appeal to function. If autobiography cannot be classified generically, then what it *does* for both the writer and reader, or for the study of literature in general for that matter, comes to the fore. Thus, Cox maintains that the study of autobiography provides for the "recovering of literature's

2. Olney, *Metaphors of Self,* 38–39.

lost ground," which he takes to be history. Janet Varner Gunn says that because autobiographers claim and take hold of the events of their lives they become "fierce with reality." Georges Gusdorf writes that autobiography is "the symbol, or parable of a consciousness in quest of its own truth." And Paul John Eakin argues that autobiography functions as a "process of self-discovery and self-creation" that ultimately points to the fictive structure of the self.[3] Like Olney's metaphorizing, then, these functions of autobiography define, in some sense, both the act and the product. At the same time, however, they are definitions that refuse to be definitions. While autobiography encompasses these functions, it is also always beyond them. As a genre autobiography would seem to "de-struct," as William V. Spanos would say, the antinomy I suggest between explicit and implicit. For Spanos, "de-struction is not . . . a nihilistic activity of thought that [portrays] its active force by levelling difference. Rather, it is, paradoxically, a positive or . . . a pro-jective interpretive activity in which thinking (*theoria*) is doing-in-the-world (*praxis*)."[4] In this sense, then, the explicit is the implicit—the work (or the study of the work), the doing-in-the-world, is the definition and vice versa. One's theory of autobiography is as much an autobiography as the work or works under scrutiny. It seems, then, that there can be no single definition of autobiography; rather, we are left only with the paradoxical and circular view that each instance of autobiography is its definition, just as each instance of criticism about autobiography projects a new and (one hopes) fruitful limitation, which is paradoxically a widening, of whatever boundaries autobiography can be said to have. What I say about autobiography could be just as readily applied to literature in general since autobiography is both more and less than literature. Current debates about the revision of the literary canon and the polysemous nature of texts point to the same lack of boundaries evidenced in autobiographical texts. The

---

3. Cox, *Recovering Literature's Lost Ground* (see especially the chapter "Recovering Literature's Lost Ground Through Autobiography"); Gunn, *Autobiography,* 17; Georges Gusdorf, "Conditions and Limits of Autobiography," in *Autobiography: Essays,* ed. Olney, 44; Eakin, *Fictions in Autobiography,* 3.

4. See Spanos, "The Indifference of *Différance*," 110, 114. For similar ideas about writing autobiography, especially with regard to the Nazi Holocaust, see Berel Lang, *Act and Idea in the Nazi Genocide* (Chicago, 1990), xii.

study of autobiography itself displays an instance of the broadening of the literary canon, of what can be defined as "literary."

In this "limitation" of the term, then, I may have realized nothing more than Olney's resistance to definition. Or perhaps I have returned to the view established in the Introduction, that autobiography is the "transformation of experience into art," a broad enough definition, to be sure, yet one that still seems a good guide for understanding the term. For such a transformation involves, as I hope to show, both limitation and possibility. It involves repetition.

AUTOBIOGRAPHY AND TIME: REPETITION

In *Autobiography: Toward a Poetics of Experience,* Janet Varner Gunn looks at the transformation of experience into art with an emphasis on the role of time. She contends that "traditional" theorists in the field of autobiography (writers such as Gusdorf and Olney) place the self in a privileged position with regard to itself and that the "ultimate expression of the self's privileged position is the Cartesian *cogito*." The result of such a placement of the self is its separation from the vicissitudes of time. She writes: "[In traditional autobiographical theory,] to avoid the contamination of time, the privacy of the true self must be made absolute. . . . Autobiography has therefore to be understood as a form of 'transcendental voyeurism'—as though the reader were getting a second-hand account of what the self, watching and overhearing itself, has seen and heard." Gunn portrays Olney, Gusdorf, and others as promoters of a Cartesian dualism whose ultimate effect on autobiographical theory "deport[s] autobiography from the country of vital experience to the desert island of Husserlian reduction or a reified textual system. At the center of their assumptions about autobiography is the hidden or ghostly self which is absolute, ineffable and timeless. Being outside the momentum of temporality and beyond the reach of language, this self cannot be said to have a past at all; it never *was;* it simply *is*."[5]

Gunn offers a corrective to what she sees as the fatal flaw to such a conception. Since she sees Olney and Gusdorf as removing the self from its involvement with time, she works from a view of the self "displayed in

5. Gunn, *Autobiography,* 7, 8.

time." Autobiography is thus viewed "not as an escape from time, but as a plunge into it; not as a self's divestment of its world involvement, but as acknowledgement of temporal experience as a vehicle of meaning."

Gunn's vision of autobiography points ultimately to a reversal of what she takes to be the implicit question traditional theory posits: "Autobiography embodies the story of Antaeus and not, as so many are ready to assume, Narcissus. Understood so, the real question of autobiography becomes *where do I belong?* not, who am I?"[6]

This idea of placement relates closely to Percy's concern with a semiotics of the self. For Percy the act of naming, which will be explored in more detail below, *places* something in a world. The self, however, is unnameable and thus without a place. Hence, Percy and Gunn share a common interest in the peculiar predicament of the self's placement and its connection to self-naming. While Gunn follows through soundly with her thesis and offers compelling readings of texts, especially *Walden,* I agree with Paul John Eakin, who maintains that her view of autobiography has more in common with Gusdorf and Olney than she admits. Eakin does not offer an analysis of these similarities; he merely suggests that Gunn would become aware of them through a closer reading of Olney. I wish to examine briefly what Eakin has left unexamined, in anticipation of my discussion of Kierkegaard's elusive category of repetition.

Gusdorf argues that man's movement away from the mythic structures that quelled the "terrors of history," the awareness of time itself, forms one of the "conditions and limits" of autobiography in the first place. When an acute awareness of historical time emerges, time becomes problematic, and the individual as individual may be compelled to write his life. The self, then, is not necessarily a fugitive from time, as Gunn suggests in her reading of Gusdorf; rather, time impels the writer forward in an attempt at self-definition, a definition, furthermore, that would have been unnecessary had the myths that provided stays for the self remained intact. For Gusdorf the multiple self-portraits of Rembrandt and Van Gogh bear witness to the "impassioned new disquiet of modern man," a disquiet brought on by their confrontation with time. The autobiographer's recollection of the past "sat-

---

6. *Ibid.*, 9, 23.

isfies a more or less anguished disquiet of the mind anxious to recover and redeem lost time in fixing it forever."[7]

Gunn also seems to overlook Olney's claim that one reason for the current interest in autobiography, as I pointed out in the Introduction, emerges from the very question of time in relation to literary texts. The shift in allegiance in recent years from the New Criticism, which espouses Stephen Dedalus' triad—"wholeness, radiance, harmony"—to what might be called "postmodern" criticism signals a new appreciation of time and clears the way for the study of autobiography, which can never satisfy the criterion of wholeness. The roots of this shift date to the 1940s, even as the tenets of New Criticism were being formulated, but at a time also, as we shall see, when the works of Søren Kierkegaard were making their way into the English-speaking world.

In "Spatial Form in Modern Literature," what has become a classic essay for postmodern theorists, Joseph Frank shows how "spatial form" composes the aesthetic of the modern period. Following Gotthold Lessing's distinction between the plastic and the literary arts in *Laokoön,* Frank suggests that what evolves in the modern period is the attempt on the part of literary artists to emulate the plastic arts. They establish an aesthetic "based on a space-logic that demands a complete re-orientation in the reader's attitude towards language. Since the primary reference of any word-group is to something inside the poem itself, language in modern poetry is really reflexive: the meaning-relationship is completed only by the simultaneous perception in space of word-groups which, when read consecutively in time, have no comprehensible relation to each other." Modern poetry's— and incidentally the novel's—creation of "images" (what Pound defined as "that which presents an intellectual and emotional complex in an instant of time") removes the very medium through which the literary arts are conveyed, namely time. While the plastic arts can be apprehended in an instant of time, Lessing contends that literature cannot because of its use of words in sequence (and because sequence implies time).

Lessing's distinction suffers, as William Spanos has shown, "in its oversimplification. . . . He is clearly wrong in his insistence that a painting or a

---

7. Eakin, *Fictions in Autobiography,* 184; Gusdorf, "Conditions and Limits," in *Autobiography: Essays,* ed. Olney, 30, 33, 35.

sculpture is perceived in an *absolute* instant of time."[8] It is restricted also, as Frank says, because Lessing developed his argument to attack the pictorial poetry and the allegorical painting of his day. Nevertheless, as Frank and Spanos make insistently clear, the "spatial" formalism of modern literature and the emphasis on the self-enclosed work that the emerging New Critics espoused lead to both the artist's and the work's removal from time. For Frank, Joyce's *A Portrait of the Artist as a Young Man* offers the best characterization of the New Critical artistic posture: "the personality of the artist, at first sight a cry or a cadence and then a fluid and lambent narrative, finally refines itself out of existence, impersonalizes itself, so to speak . . . the artist, like the God of creation, remains within or beyond or above his handiwork, invisible, refined out of existence, indifferent, paring his fingernails." It is this indifferent, transcendent, timeless attitude that Frank sees as emblematic of the "mythic" stance of modern literature, a stance that severs it from its fundamental building blocks, words in sequence—time: "past and present are seen spatially, locked in a timeless unity which, while it may accentuate surface differences, eliminates any feeling of historical sequence by the very act of juxtaposition. . . . It is this timeless world of myth, forming the common content of modern literature, which finds its appropriate aesthetic expression in spatial form."[9] His appeal to difference and time explains why his article has attained classic status and has become a sort of rallying point among those who wish to debunk New Criticism, sometimes without the finesse of Frank.

Be that as it may, Frank's insights into the "spatial form" of modern literature serve to foster a needed alternative to the view of poetry and literature as a "well-wrought urn" or "verbal icon."[10] Whereas the modern, as Frank suggests, confronts the problem of time and then retreats to the timeless world of myth, the postmodern seeks reentry into the flux of time.

I have taken this circumambient route not so much to reveal what I see as a weakness in Gunn's approach to autobiography—her emphasis on time

---

8. Frank, "Spatial Form," 229, 226; Spanos, "Modern Literary Criticism," 90.

9. Frank, "Spatial Form," 223, 233, 653.

10. See especially Bové, "Cleanth Brooks and Modern Irony," 727–59. In his first two endnotes, Bové provides a good catalog of critics who were becoming impatient with the New Critical positions.

seems entirely appropriate and in line with my own thoughts on the subject; rather, I question what I see as an oversight in her analysis of Olney and Gusdorf. For if Olney's claim about autobiography's place in the cultural moment is true, then autobiography is inextricably joined to the question of time and literature. Autobiography cannot be thoroughly encompassed by a New Critical approach to literature because that approach represses the crucial dimensions of time and change, the dimensions without which the act of autobiography would never occur. Olney does not picture the autobiographer as a fugitive from time; if there can be any single picture of the autobiographer, and for Olney this is highly unlikely, even undesirable, then it is a picture of a writer confronting and grappling with his stance in time, trying to redeem his time.

Mircea Eliade's *Cosmos and History* may add something to this discussion of myth and time, modernism and postmodernism. Eliade speaks of a "celestial double" or archetype for the navigable and habitable world of ancient culture. Every building erected, every region populated and cultivated has "an extraterrestrial archetype, be it conceived as a plan, as a form, or pure and simply as a 'double' existing at a higher cosmic level."[11] If we follow Frank and Spanos, then modernism can be seen as that literary movement that seeks to recollect such a double and thus to offer some stability to the vicissitudes of time and history. With its emphasis on mythic time (the eternal return), modern literature cannot be interested in *this* time. Rather, modernists seek to recollect what Eliade terms *illud tempus*— the privileged time of beginnings. Postmodernism, on the other hand, eschews a recollection of "sacred time" and instead looks to *this* time, *now*, as the source of possibility.

Autobiography and Percy as autobiographer both seem to straddle the fence. On the one hand, both seem postmodern because they are not primarily concerned with the past but with the now. The autobiographer retrieves the past, and is thus preoccupied with it, but always from the perspective of the present. Percy's characters, for their part, want nothing to do with the great southern archetypes of dignity and honor and duty. Instead, they come to a realization of the possibility of acting now. Allie says

11. Mircea Eliade, *Cosmos and History: The Myth of the Eternal Return*, trans. Willard R. Trask (Princeton, 1971), 9.

in *The Second Coming:* "What was my (your, our) discovery? That I could *act.* I was *free* to act. . . . How does one ever make the discovery that one can actually be free to act for oneself? I don't know. I don't even know how many people, if any, do it" (*SC,* 40). For both Percy and autobiography the past serves primarily as a repository of foreclosed potentialities. The possibility for action in time depends on these potentialities becoming actual.

Although Percy would not agree entirely with Spanos' postmodern destructive project, I cannot help seeing similarities between the two. Percy's "open" literature opposes the mythic closure of modernism. The narrator of *The Thanatos Syndrome* warns against such closure: "TV has screwed up millions of people with their little rounded-off stories. Because that is not the way life is. Life is fits and starts, mostly fits" (*TS,* 75). Like autobiography, then, Percy's works resist a closure that life itself does not provide, except in death. His works embrace no celestial double but engage in the labyrinth of now—time and language and consciousness. What interests me about Spanos and his relation to the work of Percy (and, of course, their relation to autobiography) is his use of Heideggerian retrieval or repetition, which has its source in Kierkegaard's category of the same name. Percy was, of course, a devoted reader of both Heidegger and Kierkegaard. Although Spanos divests repetition of its religious significance (a step that restricts the very possibilities he hails), he nevertheless points to an understanding of the term with regard to both its philosophical and literary implications.

I return, then, to the question of time and autobiography, the question that launched me on this excursion in the first place. Both Gusdorf and Olney see the autobiographer's desire to redeem time as a prime motive for writing. I have cited Gusdorf's reference to this redemption: The autobiographer's recollection of the past "satisfies a more or less anguished disquiet of the mind anxious to recover and redeem lost time in fixing it forever." Olney makes the same claim, although more emphatically. He writes: "To redeem the time is one of the autobiographer's prime motives, perhaps *the* prime motive—perhaps, indeed, the only real motive of the autobiographer." This comment comes in the context of T. S. Eliot's line from *Four Quartets.* "If all time is eternally present / All time is unredeemable." Olney shows the sense in which different understandings of *bios* can render time either absolutely past or eternally present:

> If *bios* is the historical course of a life, then at any given present moment of that life it is necessarily true that all things have flowed and that nothing remains: "is" has been transformed into "was" and has thereby been drained of all vitality, of all reality, of all life; "what was" no longer composes a part of *ta onta,* the present, the sum of things that are now existing or that are now being. If, on the other hand, *bios* is taken as the vital principle or the unique spark—life as transformed by being lived through this one-of-a-kind medium—then there is nothing but "is": there is no "was" in the picture and there is clearly no relation between "is" and "was." [12]

In either case, time becomes unredeemable. The autobiographer redeems his time through the interplay of past and present, which takes place in memory. Although Olney proposes different versions of redemption (some not involving memory at all, and some so transforming memory as to make it unrecognizable), he suggests that the "most complex resolution of the autobiographer's dilemma" takes place in memory:

> Time carries us away from all of our earlier states of being; memory recalls those earlier states—but it does so only as a function of present consciousness: we can recall what we were only from the complex perspective of what we are, which means that we may very well be recalling something that we never were at all. In the act of remembering the past in the present, the autobiographer imagines into existence another person, another world, and surely it is *not* the same, in any real sense, as that past world that does not, under any circumstances, nor however much we may wish it, now exist. [13]

Olney's insistence on the possibility of "recalling something that we never were at all" or bringing into existence "another person, another world" seems to echo part of what Spanos, following Heidegger, would call the movement of retrieval or repetition. (I say "part of" because the future—"anticipatory resolution"—also comes into play for Heidegger and Kierkegaard, as I will discuss below.) This retrieval seems to be a version of redemption, similar to yet different from the one Olney suggests. It is a redemption in its most primitive meaning of "recovering that of which possession had been lost," as Nathan Scott puts it. For if a recovery occurs, there is a sense in which it brings into existence another person and world,

12. Olney, "Some Versions," in *Autobiography: Essays,* ed. Olney, 240, 239–40.
13. *Ibid.,* 241.

since the condition of loss means an absence or unawareness of what is lost. Repetition, then, becomes an originary experience—the origin, in the case of autobiography, of the person brought into existence through the act of writing one's life, in whatever form.[14]

Spanos approaches the question of retrieval or repetition from the perspective of a hermeneutics of literary texts, which, in turn, derives from Heidegger's hermeneutic circle.[15] The following note, which includes a footnote from *Being and Time,* helps to clarify both Spanos' and Heidegger's understanding of the term:

> The translators of *Being and Time,* Macquarrie and Robinson, translate *"Wiederholen"* as "Repetition" (others, as "Retrieval") and add in a footnote:
>
>> this English word is hardly adequate to express Heidegger's meaning. Etymologically, "wiederholen" means "to fetch again"; in modern German usage, however, this is expressed by the cognate separable verb "wieder . . . holen," while "wiederholen" means simply "to repeat" or "do over again." Heidegger departs from both these meanings, as he is careful to point out. For him, "wiederholen" does not mean either a mere mechanical repetition or an attempt to reconstitute the physical past; it means rather an attempt to go back to the past and retrieve former *possibilities,* which are thus "explicitly handed down" or "transmitted."[16]

Heidegger writes of repetition with respect to "Dasein," the being that is there to question its own being, that always already has a vague sense of being, and thereby reopens the question of ontology. His entire methodology, as it is set up in the opening sections of *Being and Time,* calls for a repetition or retrieval of the question of being. Spanos, however, applies the category to literary criticism. For Heidegger Dasein confronts the necessity of interpreting its own being, and the act of interpretation itself, of

14. Scott, *The Broken Center,* 74; see F. H. Heinemann, "Origin and Repetition," *Review of Metaphysics,* IV (1950–51), 201–14.

15. I will refer primarily to "Heidegger, Kierkegaard, and the Hermeneutic Circle." I have consulted a number of other sources on the question of Kierkegaard and postmodernism in general and repetition in particular, to which I do not directly refer. These sources have, nevertheless, helped me to understand this elusive term and its author, and they are listed in the bibliography.

16. Spanos, "Hermeneutic Circle," 481, note 9; see also Martin Heidegger, *Being and Time,* trans. John Macquarrie and Edward Robinson (New York, 1962), 437.

course, falls into the domain of literary criticism. Just as Heidegger de-structs (or de-structures) the Western metaphysical tradition—which has imposed an interpretation from without, from a standpoint beyond or after the physical (*metá-tá-physiká*), a standpoint devoid of temporality—to re-trieve new possibilities for Dasein, and hence for the question of being, so Spanos through his application of the Heideggerian method, that is, through his emphasis on time, retrieves new possibilities for the act of lit-erature.[17] He writes: "I want to suggest a hermeneutics that remembers or retrieves the occasion—the time—that engaged and interested [literary ac-tivity] and, in so doing, reactivated the ongoing and interminable explora-tive process." It is so-called postmodern literature that opens itself best to this hermeneutic activity: "Postmodern literature . . . becomes a kind of writing that is 'grounded' in an ungrounded understanding of being, a kind of 'de-structive' writing, as it were, which remains marginal up to the middle of this century, but which increasingly thereafter becomes the cen-tral preoccupation of dramatists, poets, and novelists."[18]

It is important to emphasize, again, that this de-structive method is not, for Spanos (or for Heidegger), a nihilistic movement—one that wan-tonly destroys without any possibility of renewal. It is a method, rather, that *dis-closes* what has been *fore-closed* by the metaphysical tradition. Whereas interpretation in that tradition has worked from an atemporal, closed circle—a repetition that ceaselessly and mechanically repeats the same thing—Spanos works from Heidegger's hermeneutic circle:

> To put it positively, the hermeneutic circle is, paradoxically, *a liberating move-ment, an opening towards being*. It is finally, to use the important term that Hei-degger borrows from Kierkegaard, a "repetition" or "retrieval" (*Wiederholen*), a process of dis-covering and re-membering the primordial temporality of being and thus of the truth as *a-letheia* (unhiddenness), which metaphysical under-standing and interpretation, . . . in *closing time off*—in coercing temporality into spatial icon (the circle)—and hardening this closure into "tradition," covers over and forgets. . . . Retrieval or repetition, that is, is neither a process of re-cognizing a (historical) text in the tradition for its own sake; nor is it a process

---

17. Spanos uses the term *metaphysics* to his own ends. For Aristotle, the term referred only to the chronology of his writing. Thus, metaphysics signified the material he wrote *after* he had written about the physical universe.

18. Spanos, *Repetitions,* 6, 8.

of re-collecting an absolute or privileged origin (logos as presence) as agency of judging a text in the tradition. It is rather a discovering of beginnings in the sense of rendering the present interpreter . . . a *homo viator,* of bringing him into an original, a *care*ful explorative (open) relationship (a relationship of "anticipatory resoluteness") with the being of a text in the tradition.[19]

I have quoted Spanos at length because I find this his most concise statement of the de-structive project that destroys only to open up new possibilities—the clearest statement of his use of repetition. Nevertheless, the quotation seems to call for some further clarification, something I can only half-ironically and indirectly, half-seriously and directly, provide by invoking Kierkegaard, who remains a very slippery character, and whose book, *Repetition,* gives only "hints and guesses, / Hints followed by guesses" as to what the term might signify.[20] I approach this task fully aware that indirection, as Kierkegaard knew, is the only genuine way to fathom this elusive category, since it belongs, as Stephen Crites points out, to the existential sphere, and that once reduced to the sphere of the aesthetic, it loses its potency. The power and, of course, the difficulty of Kierkegaard's pseudonymous aesthetic works result from the paradoxical attempt to render the existential by means of the aesthetic. As Crites observes, "these communications in which Kierkegaard set out to evoke the existential categories in their opposition to the aesthetic were themselves self-consciously aesthetic works." Kierkegaard actually developed his writings around three spheres— the aesthetic, the ethical, and the religious. Crites argues that since there is an "exfoliation" of dimensions within the major stages, it is best to approach them under the broader headings of aesthetic and existential, the first comprising the realm of the interesting (pleasure or displeasure), the second the realm of interest (concern, care).

In this sense Percy absorbed more from Kierkegaard than simply his thought. His novels can be read as incorporating a similar narrative strategy, an attempt, as Crites points out about Kierkegaard, not so much to disseminate knowledge as "to draw the reader into a consideration of his personal life." Thus, both Kierkegaard's and Percy's works, while aesthetic

19. Spanos, "Hermeneutic Circle," 462 (his emphasis).
20. Quoting T. S. Eliot, "The Dry Salvages."

fabrications, offer themselves as "existence communications," as having to do with the existential realm.[21]

Kierkegaard presents his readers with a drama enacted by the various pseudonyms he sets on stage: Judge William (a representative of the ethical stage) urges the young A (the aesthete of *Either/Or*) to choose; Johannes de Silentio (*Fear and Trembling*) seeks the Knight of Faith, whose movement he is unable to imitate in his own life; Constantin Constantius (*Repetition*) sets up an "interesting" experiment of repetition only to have his hopes dashed, while the young poet (his "nameless correspondent") achieves a repetition without too much effort. This Kierkegaardian drama is not intended to bring stasis or rest. Nor does it exist as an object to be contemplated from a distance. Because it wants its reader to confront his personal life, its primary aim is to bring the reader to a point of decision, to action, or as Spanos says above, into a *care*ful relationship with being, a relationship possible only in time. It is only through action in time, after all, that repetition is possible.[22] Kierkegaard's pseudonymous works, then, like those of his philosophical successor, are both "art" and "act"; they point to the existential by means of the aesthetic.

Just as Kierkegaard's ostensible purpose behind his work focused on his relationship with Regine Olson, so Percy once commented to Martin Luschei that writing *The Moviegoer* was "better therapy than three years of psychoanalysis."[23] In this light both Tolson's and Allen's contention that Percy's fiction repeats the conflicts he had with the "absent mother" and with "fathers" finds justification. Yet Percy's concern with repetition, like Kierkegaard's, moves beyond himself to the life of the culture in which he found himself and to the very act of writing. Both men confront themselves in their writing, yet in so doing they also confront their readers with their

---

21. Stephen Crites, "Pseudonymous Authorship as Art and as Act," in *Kierkegaard: A Collection of Critical Essays,* ed. Josiah Thompson (Garden City, N.Y., 1972), 205. See also *In the Twilight of Christendom,* (Chambersburg, Pa., 1972) and "The Author and the Authorship: Recent Kierkegaard Literature," *Journal of the American Academy of Religion,* XXXVIII (1970), 37–54; Crites, "Author and Authorship," 39; Crites, "Pseudonymous Authorship," in *Kierkegaard,* 217–18.

22. Crites, *Twilight,* 65.

23. Martin Luschei, *The Sovereign Wayfarer: Walker Percy's Diagnosis of the Malaise* (Baton Rouge, 1972), 16.

own action or inaction in time. Both see writing as evincing not a mythic double but concerned action in time.

Kierkegaard's *Repetition* is cast from the point of view of Constantin Constantius. The book begins with his "report" after meeting a young poet who has fallen in love, but who does not love the girl for her own sake, only for the role she plays as his muse. The poet becomes increasingly depressed, and he seeks something to assuage his melancholy; his first efforts are unsuccessful. Constantin goes on to tell of his own humorous attempts at repetition by returning to Berlin and trying to see that everything is the same as it had been on his last trip. This report is then followed by letters from the poet, who has abandoned his fiancée and who begins the movement of repetition, at first deepening his melancholy, through reading the Book of Job. The nameless poet is granted a repetition, paradoxically, when he learns of his love's engagement to another man. The work ends with Constantin's addressing his reader directly with reflections on the whole affair. Although the poet attains repetition and Constantin does not, the nature of the movement remains obscure. The book revolves around its subject without defining it directly. As Richard M. Griffith notes: "If I, who use the word repetition, pause to reflect, I despair that I speak nonsense. . . . Repetition feeds upon time which is its poison. . . . Fortunately, [Kierkegaard], like Socrates, said the same thing over and over again, but always differently. Thus, in a wider sense, what he said about repetition fills some thirty volumes."[24] One of the hints we are given comes at the very beginning of the book, where Constantin compares repetition to recollection:

> Say what you will, this question will play a very important role in modern philosophy, for *repetition* is a crucial expression for what "recollection" was to the Greeks. Just as they taught that all knowing is a recollecting, modern philosophy will teach that all life is a repetition. . . . Repetition and recollection are the same movement, except in opposite directions, for what is recollected has been, is repeated backward, whereas genuine repetition is recollected forward. Repetition, therefore, if it is possible, makes a person happy, whereas recollection makes him unhappy.[25]

24. Richard M. Griffith, "Repetition: Constantin (S.) Constantius," *Journal of Existential Psychiatry,* II (1962), 438, 440.

25. Kierkegaard, *Fear and Trembling/Repetition,* 131.

This distinction between recollection and repetition, although insistent and central (because of Constantin's "constant" reference to it at the beginning of his enigmatic narrative), remains rather cryptic. The situation is partially clarified when the pseudonymous author, after he meets the poet in despair over the love affair, tells the reader that the poet's problem is one of recollection: "His mistake was incurable, and his mistake was that he stood at the end instead of at the beginning, but such a mistake is and remains a person's downfall."

To say that the poet stands at the end of the relationship suggests that he has cast himself forward in imagination to a time when he and his love are old and gray, sitting around the hearth, reading bedtime stories to their grandchildren. Such a casting forward negates the present (the actual living through) of the affair. It ends the matter before it has actually begun: "If anyone can join in conversation about recollection's love, [the poet] can. Recollection has the great advantage that it begins with the loss; the reason it is safe and secure is that it has nothing to lose."[26] The poet, Constantin tells the reader, has cast himself clear out of his involvement with time. His recollection is not the "recollection forward" that is repetition, but rather the placing of the self at an advantaged viewpoint (outside itself) so that it might gain an overall view of the affair (its end) before it has actually begun. The poet is unhappy, to be sure, but he is secure in his unhappiness because he has taken no real chances, has made no choices in time. Thus, he has nothing to lose. It is already lost in the recollection.

Yet one has to be wary of Constantin's point of view. One of the central ironies of the book, after all, arises from the fact that while Constantin writes of the nature of repetition, he never attains the movement. And whereas the poet cannot explain the "thunderstorm" that happens to him, he is granted a repetition. Part of the reason for this resides in the pseudonym itself. Since Constantin, the observer and reporter of the affair, is the "constant" one, he is removed from the flux, the momentum of time. He has adopted, as Spanos has noted, an observer's stance, a metaphysical viewpoint, the constancy of recollection. He projects, then, his own stance upon the poet. As "reporter," he can only write about the movement, an essentially aesthetic (recollective) activity, but he is unable to make the

26. *Ibid.*, 137, 136.

movement himself. The poet, on the other hand, because he really does suffer (despite Constantin's preferred interpretation) and because he turns to the Book of Job (a book about a legitimate exception), "step by step" and "educated by life . . . now discovers repetition."[27] Or, if we grant Constantin his interpretation and say that the poet really is lost in recollective despair, with everything this situation implies, then the poet nevertheless breaks out of that recollection into the birth of repetition. In either case, Constantin remains all the more impoverished for his constancy, for his recollective posture.

Yet repetition remains nonetheless elusive. Further into the work, Constantin gives us more hints and guesses as to what he means by the term:

> The dialectic of repetition is easy, for that which is repeated has been—otherwise it could not be repeated—but the very fact that it has been makes the repetition into something new. When the Greeks said that all knowing is recollecting, they said that all existence, which is, has been; when one says that life is a repetition, one says: actuality, which has been, now comes into existence. If one does not have the category of recollection or of repetition, all life dissolves into an empty, meaningless noise. Recollection is the pagan view of life, repetition is the modern; repetition is the *interest* of metaphysics and also the interest upon which metaphysics comes to grief.[28]

Now if "time is the moving image of eternity," as Plato says in the *Timaeus,* then one's existence in time can claim little value outside of the constant effort to cast off its shackles and so enter the immutable world of forms. One's existence becomes the struggle to recollect what one already knows (but what has been forgotten) because one is himself a moving image of eternity who "has been." But this recollection demands as its terminus the stasis that is eternity, a return to originary time. It demands not that one enter with interest his own time, but rather a disinterested entry into that mythic time (*illo tempore*), which constitutes the origin of the cosmos, as Eliade would say. This is, to put it simplistically, the pagan view of a life of recollection as Constantin seems to see it, and it is the poet's stance, in the view of the pseudonym, toward his love affair at the beginning of the book. It is the "aesthetic" strategy of dealing with time, the stance that be-

27. *Ibid.,* 304.
28. *Ibid.,* 149.

gins with loss. It is also the stance that Frank and Spanos see as emblematic of the literature and criticism of modernism. For as Frank has shown, modernism seeks the stasis of myth, and myth, as Nathan Scott writes, "is that form in which the imagination undertakes to grasp the eternal present, the Time which is above and outside of time, the Great Time, in which all the concrete times and seasons of life eternally return to the same." It is interesting to note that, besides Scott, several writers on biblical aspects of time point to an essential difference between the Greeks' understanding of time and that of ancient Israel. The Greeks, as James Muilenburg writes, had a tendency to reduce time to form, to spatialize it. The Israelites, however, had no "concept" of time; rather, it was lived: "In Israel the mystery and meaning of time is not resolved by appeal to the cosmic world of space."[29]

If recollection is the "pagan" view of life, repetition is the postmodern view. It is a movement not out of time into an eternity that has been forgotten, and thus in need of being remembered, but rather a reduplication of the paradoxical entry of eternity into time (the infinite into the finite). As such, its primary thrust is not backward, but forward. It is not the stance of loss, but of gain.[30] One attains himself—one becomes—by means of a *care*ful, forward-looking interest that makes decisions in time. It is the "existential" strategy for dealing with human temporality. Although time is "dread-ful" for both the aesthete and the existentialist (in the sense, as Crites puts it, that it sets forth infinite possibilities, freedom), time is not something from which to flee. It is, rather, the place where dread can beckon one to himself. Spanos points out that for Kierkegaard and Heidegger, dread is an objectless condition. It is the feeling of not being at home (*unheimlicheit*), which, in despair and inauthenticity, Dasein seeks to objec-

29. Scott, *The Broken Center,* 46; James Muilenburg, "The Biblical View of Time," *The Harvard Theological Review,* LIV (1961), 221–52. See also Robert Johann, S.J., "Charity and Time," *Cross Currents,* IX (1959), 140–49; Paul S. Minear, "Thanksgiving as a Synthesis of the Temporal and Eternal," *Anglican Theological Review,* XXXVIII (1956), 4–14, and "The Time of Hope in the New Testament," *Scottish Journal of Theology,* VI (1953), 337–61. With regard to Percy's "biblical anthropology" see Lewis A. Lawson, "The Cross and the Delta: Walker Percy's Anthropology," in *Walker Percy: Novelist and Philosopher,* ed. Jan Nordby Gretlund and Karl-Heinz Westarp (Jackson, 1991), 3–12.

30. See Michael Sprinker, "Fictions of the Self: The End of Autobiography," in *Autobiography: Essays,* ed. Olney, 330.

tify, that is, to convert to fear, which has an object. It is this uncanniness that leads Dasein to interest, and Spanos emphasizes that term's double significance: "to be between" and "to be a matter of concern."[31] Repetition as the "*interest* of metaphysics and also the interest upon which metaphysics comes to grief" suggests, then, that the proper movement of metaphysics is not from a disinterested stance "beyond the physical," wherein time and space (the individual) hold no sway, but rather from a concern within it. "To be between" the finite and the infinite, for example, is the human condition of temporality, what the self already is. Without such interest metaphysics founders because the self becomes, not what it *is,* but, as Crites puts it, a "deficient polarization of spirit."[32] As Percy puts it, the self flies either to the angelic infinite, which too often has been the case in metaphysics, or it sinks itself in the finite and takes up its home as a beast among beasts. In the movement of repetition the individual becomes, then, what he already is through concerned action in time. Spanos summarizes the movement with respect to the individual in this way:

> In "recollecting forward," repetition relies precisely on the *interest,* the intentionality of *inter esse,* of the unique, the existential individual as being-in-the-world, for its access into the meaning of being. It is not an objective mode, a contemplative act from without *aeterno modo.* It is, rather, a "subjective," a Care-ful, mode, in which the singular, or in Kierkegaard's preferred term, the *exceptional* interpreter (as opposed to a universal observer like Constantius himself) is guided beyond the present by the intimation of spirit (the primordial question of being) residing in his "memory." As such, repetition is *both* a mnemonic and an anticipatory—i.e. a de-structive and ek-static—movement.[33]

The "memory" that Spanos here refers to is precisely the vague sense of being that every individual always and already has, according to Heidegger. Repetition, then, is the movement in which this vague sense of being "stands out" from destructive chaos yet resists angelic form. It is between the pure form of recollection ("spatial form") and no form whatsoever.

31. Crites, "Pseudonymous Authorship," in *Kierkegaard,* 205ff; Spanos, "Modern Literary Criticism," 87, 102; Spanos, "Hermeneutic Circle," 464.

32. Kierkegaard develops a dialectic between the infinite and the finite in *The Sickness unto Death,* ed. and trans. Howard V. Hong and Edna H. Hong (Princeton, 1980), 33ff; Crites, *Twilight,* 68.

33. Spanos, "Hermeneutic Circle," 465.

The difference between repetition and recollection, finally, is a difference between an entry into the temporality of human existence or a flight from it. Crites provides a good summary of this fundamental difference in terms of the aesthetic and existential: "Both the aesthetic strategy and the existential movement proceed from the impasse created by our peculiarly human temporality. The aesthetic strategy, however, proceeds by negating that temporality, the existential movement by intensifying it and through passion giving it a form that is itself temporalized. . . . Aesthetic apprehension wrests ideal possibility out of the actual through recollection. Existential movement projects a chosen possibility into the real world through action."[34]

Crites's observation that the existential movement of repetition "gives a form that is itself temporalized" could just as well be read as "giving a temporized form." For what repetition allows is a continual recasting of the form that the self shall inhabit, not in the sense of grasping after one possibility and then another—that would be the aesthetic stance—but rather in the sense that the possibility that is chosen (or given) does not close off the self in a definite and mechanical replication of form, but rather opens the self to endless possibilities within that form. Form, then, is not imposed from above, as in the traditional metaphysical posture; it is not something that strives for stasis. Rather, it opens from below, if you will, from a stance between the finite and the infinite, which the self already is. Repetition, then, returns one to himself in such a way that a birth of the self occurs: new possibilities are projected because former ones have been disclosed, and former possibilities are disclosed because the future enters with its new, indeterminate ones.

In repetition the self becomes the clearest path to the universal. The self, the "exception" for Kierkegaard, inhabits the universal, not as a slave, but as a co-creator who becomes. Toward the end of *Repetition*, in a letter addressed to "My dear Reader," Constantin acknowledges the relation between the exception and the universal. The "exception" is a category Johannes de Silentio develops in *Fear and Trembling*, published the same day as *Repetition*, with regard to Abraham, who surpassed the ethical, *i.e.*, universal, injunction against murder in his willingness to undergo trial or ordeal

34. Crites, "Pseudonymous Authorship," in *Kierkegaard*, 214.

by making a religious sacrifice of Isaac. In *Repetition,* the exception is Job, who despite his friends' claims to the contrary (made on the basis of universal knowledge), is really not guilty and whose entire story can be seen as a test by God. It is by virtue of these exceptions that repetition is possible for the story's poet, who is himself an exception (by virtue of his ordeal with his fiancée), although only a "transitional" one from the aesthetic through the ethical to the religious: "Such an exception is a poet, who constitutes the transition to the truly aristocratic exceptions, to the religious exceptions." This short recapitulation of Kierkegaard's three stages (the aesthetic/poetic, the ethical/aristocratic, and the religious), which, as I have pointed out (following Crites), can best be understood as the aesthetic and the existential, helps clarify the relation between the exception and the universal without which repetition would be impossible. For true repetition, as the poet says, is "eternity"—the paradoxical dwelling of the infinite in the finite, and thus an essentially religious category. It is, as Crites observes, a reduplication of the Incarnation: "if *the eternal* entered time in that past event, we meet it [in repetition] as the infinite possibility of the future. In the language of recent theology, the Christ-event is the eschatological event."[35] This indwelling of the infinite in the finite represents the ultimate hope Percy strives for in his works.

On this facet of repetition I disagree with Spanos. For he would balk at any talk of Incarnation, since it is borrowed, as he might say, from the "archival, logos-as-presence language of the institutional church." Yet Incarnation for Kierkegaard, as Crites points out, is not a call to an intellectual contemplation of doctrine; its nature as absolute paradox (of eternity entering time) cannot be grasped by the intellect. Incarnation, like repetition, remains elusive. And like repetition, Incarnation is the summons to decision by which the individual begins the act of self-definition. Spanos seems to see the term only in light of a doctrinal assent to the dual natures of Christ, human and divine. And yet his writing on repetition seems to me wholly in line with Crites's and Kierkegaard's understanding of Incarna-

---

35. Kierkegaard, *Fear and Trembling/Repetition,* 228, 221; Crites, *Twilight,* 81. For a treatment of Percy and the eschaton, see Gary M. Ciuba, *Walker Percy: Books of Revelations* (Athens, 1991).

tion—as a call to decision. That is why I continue to call on his help in dealing with the term repetition.

There is a sense, too, in which repetition should not be connected with Incarnation, since much of Kierkegaard's writing was against Christendom, against the very domesticated version of Christianity that Christendom implies. Thus, the philosophical word "repetition" would seem better suited to an age that already thinks it understands Incarnation or, better, thinks that all it has to do is understand it.

Kierkegaard's poet does not make this fuller movement of repetition; rather, his is merely transitional. Nevertheless, it is a repetition. Through his suffering and his reading of Job, he makes the initial steps of the religious movement, in the etymological sense of religion: a re-binding, a re-connecting, a re-joining. His time is redeemed. Because Constantin remains on the aesthetic sphere, on the other hand, he can only create a farce of repetition, his failed attempt at it through his return to Berlin. He can never be the exception because he cannot "repeat" his life. Although he is capable of expressing the universal, art and act do not coalesce for him. He stands above and outside his work as reporter, so he cannot act in time as does the "exceptional" poet. The relation between the universal and the exceptional, then, is a good expression of repetition, but also a superb statement of the act of autobiography:

> The exception also thinks the universal in that he thinks himself through; he works for the universal in that he works himself through; he explains the universal in that he explains himself. Consequently, the exception explains the universal and himself, and if one really wants to study the universal, one only needs to look around for a legitimate exception; he discloses everything far more clearly than the universal itself. . . . There are exceptions. If they cannot be explained, then the universal cannot be explained, either. Generally, the difficulty is not noticed because one thinks the universal not with passion but with a comfortable superficiality. The exception, however, thinks the universal with intense passion.[36]

Thus Johannes de Silentio says that he can understand Hegel, whose philosophical system "is supposed to be difficult to understand," yet he cannot

---

36. Kierkegaard, *Fear and Trembling/Repetition,* 22; for more on the universal and the exception, see Barrett J. Mandel, "Full of Life Now," in *Autobiography: Essays,* ed. Olney, 69.

fathom the figure of Abraham, who, according to the age, "is a small matter." Hegel treats the universal without passion, with "comfortable superficiality." But Abraham, as the exceptional, receives the universal after he had surpassed it in his willingness to sacrifice Isaac.

In *Repetition,* this passion is not only the poet's suffering for the pain he causes his beloved, but also the interest with which he questions his own existence: "One sticks a finger into the ground to smell what country one is in; I stick my finger into the world—it has no smell. Where am I? What does it mean to say: the world? . . . Who tricked me into this whole thing and leaves me standing here? Who am I? How did I get into the world?"[37] This concern heralds not only the radical dislocation that arrives in our postmodern world, but also the care with which the autobiographer questions his own time and place. For the two questions, "Where am I?" and "Who am I?" constitute the autobiographical dilemma, whether one takes as the prototypical autobiographical movement the story of Narcissus or the story of Anteaus, as Janet Varner Gunn suggests. In either case it is the writer's reckoning with time, with a sense of loss or deprivation, which leads him or her to transform experience into art, with the hope, as the poet notes, that repetition will occur: "I am myself again. The 'self' that someone else would not pick up off the street I have once again. The split that was in my being is healed; I am unified again. The anxieties of sympathy that were sustained and nourished by my pride are no longer there to disintegrate and disrupt. Is there not, then, a repetition? Did I not get everything double? Did I not get myself again and precisely in such a way that I might have a double sense of its meaning? . . . I am born to myself."[38] The poet's ability to express his movement in words suggests not only his junction of art and act, but also the doubleness of repetition itself. The text, the writing, doubles his experience, not according to one of Eliade's "celestial archetypes," but according to his being in time now. This is the sense in which autobiographers seek to redeem the time, and this is the sense in which autobiography can be understood as repetition.[39]

37. Kierkegaard, *Fear and Trembling/Repetition,* 32–33, 200.

38. *Ibid.,* 220–21.

39. For more on this "doubling" see Gusdorf, "Conditions and Limits," in *Autobiography: Essays,* ed. Olney, 43.

Kierkegaard, of course, wrote much of his philosophy as a response to what he saw as the universal, speculative, Hegelian system, which is the ultimate expression of the Cartesian body/mind split. Although he had a great respect for Hegel, and although he applies the Hegelian dialectic in his own works, he applies it to the one entity that Hegel left out of his philosophy—the individual. For Hegel's is a philosophy of the universal, the System, and such a system can encompass everything from above (from the end) without worrying at all about the existing individual: "It is from this side . . . that objection must be made to modern philosophy; not that it has a mistaken presupposition, but that it has a comical presupposition, occasioned by its having forgotten, in a sort of world-historical absent-mindedness, what it means to be a human being. Not indeed, what it means to be a human being in general; for this is the sort of thing that one might even induce a speculative philosopher to agree to; but what it means that you and I and he are human beings, each one for himself."[40] Without the individual, for Kierkegaard, there cannot be faith, and without faith, there cannot be an individual. Just as the existing individual cannot be subsumed by the System, by objective knowledge, neither can faith in Christianity. For Christianity is not so much a matter of knowledge—it is not a System—although the philosophy of the age tries to make it so; rather, it is passionate inwardness that paradoxically turns one outward. And such passion belongs strictly to the individual. It is Abraham, not Hegel, who is the stumbling block.

When the poet attains repetition, then, he moves out of his recollective (speculative) stance that separates mind and body, thought and existence, eternity and time, the infinite and the finite. The split is healed. He re-enters (retrieves/repeats) what he already is. This is not to say that he is a Christian in the full Kierkegaardian sense of Christianity; it is to say only that he has made the first movement back to himself, a movement that demands repetition in order to reach the threshold of faith, for Kierkegaard the highest expression of individuality.

Similarly, to say that autobiographers repeat their existence is not to say that they are all Christians, a ludicrous assertion. Rather, it suggests that

40. Søren Kierkegaard, *Concluding Unscientific Postscript,* trans. David F. Swenson and Walter Lowrie (Princeton, 1941), 109.

the autobiographical posture is the same as that of repetition. The autobiographer does not remove himself from himself *aeterno modo*. Even St. Augustine and Newman, who write autobiographies of conversion, and who thus stand at the end of their movement rather than the beginning, nevertheless embody the repetitive posture. St. Augustine, incidentally, says he writes *sub specie aeternitatis* (apparently from the recollective posture), but he certainly exemplifies the repetitive nature of autobiography in his reflections on time and memory in Books X and XI. And although Newman once stated that his doctrinal struggles ended when he entered the Roman Catholic Church, he also said life in time meant change. The autobiographer, then, since he is an existing individual at the present time of his writing, since he is still trying to fathom and redeem his time by means of writing, cannot know the end of his story. He writes from his middle state (*inter esse*) in an attempt to define himself, to become the single individual for himself and for his readers. He tries, that is, not so much to recollect another time (*illud tempus*) but to retrieve the present time, to make it habitable. He combines art and act in a form that does not close off the possibilities for existence, but rather closes the split only to open possibilities. That form, of course, is the book that reaches an end that repeats or retrieves a beginning—not timelessly, but in time. It is not the eternal present that the autobiographer seeks, but simply the present.

AUTOBIOGRAPHY, THE NOVEL, AND PERCY

Under the entry for Walker Percy in *The History of Southern Literature,* Lewis A. Lawson, perhaps the best of Percy's students, writes that Percy "has not removed his name from the physicians' register" because "he continues to diagnose and prescribe."[41] The first book of criticism written on Percy, in fact, emphasizes his stance as diagnostician, Martin Luschei's *The Sovereign Wayfarer: Walker Percy's Diagnosis of the Malaise.* And a short sample of some titles Percy gives his own essays indicates that he views both the novel's and the novelist's role as diagnostic, as an "instrument for exploration and discovery" (*Signposts,* 219): "The State of the Novel: Dying Art

41. Louis D. Rubin, Jr., *et al.,* eds., *The History of Southern Literature* (Baton Rouge, 1985), 509.

or New Science?"; "Diagnosing the Modern Malaise"; "Physician as Novelist." But the novelist is not only a physician; Percy also likens him to a wounded man "who has a better view of the battle than those still shooting." Or, better still, "the novelist is less like a prophet than he is like the canary that coal miners used to take down into the shaft to test the air. When the canary gets unhappy, utters plaintive cries, and collapses, it may be time for the miners to surface and think things over" (*MB*, 101).

Percy's concern with diagnosis and his figures of speech, of course, presuppose a radical disease. His view of himself as writer provides him a chance to "utter plaintive cries" so that his readers might begin to "think things over" and thus get a handle on the malady. The cries have to be uttered, for "it is only when one sees that something is wrong that one can diagnose it, point it out and name it, toward the end that the patient might at least have hope, and even in the end get well" (*Signposts*, 196).

But why is there such desperation in the postmodern world? Why is there a need to "utter plaintive cries"? What is the root of this malaise? Is it a totally new phenomenon or does it have its origins in an earlier age? Why is the novelist well-suited to write about it? That is, what is it about the novel that gives it such diagnostic potential? And how is all of this related to the question of autobiography and repetition?

As in the first section of this chapter, it may be useful to begin with a limiting of terms, especially *postmodern*. For if I wish to place Percy in the company of postmodern writers and theorists, then some clear notion of the term should be available. Fortunately, Percy provides his own definition:

> To state the matter as plainly as possible, I would echo a writer like Guardini who says simply that the modern world has ended, the world, that is, of the past two or three hundred years, which we think of as having been informed by the optimism of the scientific revolution, rational humanism, and that Western cultural entity which until this century it has been more or less accurate to describe as Christendom. I am not telling you anything you don't already know when I say that the optimism of this age began to crumble with the onset of the catastrophes of the twentieth century. If one had to set a date of the beginning of the end of the modern world, 1914 would be as good as any, because it was then that Western man, the beneficiary of precisely this scientific revolution and Christian ethic, began with great skill and energy to destroy himself.
>
> (*Signposts*, 208)

Thus, the postmodern world can be understood only in relation to the modern one that preceded it, characterized by the exuberance brought on by rational humanism and the scientific revolution, the waning of Christendom.

It is entirely germane that the modern period so described also witnessed the rise of both the novel and autobiography. And this was not only the age of the scientific revolution, but also of the American and French revolutions. I have already cited Georges Gusdorf's superb essay "Conditions and Limits of Autobiography" with regard to autobiography's relation to time. Autobiography arises, it will be remembered, when the mythic structures that held the terrors of history at bay broke down. Gusdorf reiterates this point when he contends that autobiography emerged when "the traditional communal life" broke down and "the individual qua individual became important." He continues: "At the cost of a cultural revolution humanity must have emerged from the mythic framework of traditional teachings and must have entered the perilous domain of history. The man who takes the trouble to tell of himself knows that the present differs from the past and that it will not be repeated in the future."

James Cox corroborates Gusdorf's comments about revolution. It is "interesting to note," Cox writes, "that its [the word's (*i.e., autobiography's*)] appearance comes just after the age of revolution, when the modern self was being liberated as well as defined. At the time of the revolutions, Franklin and Rousseau were writing their memoirs and confessions, respectively."[42] This paradoxical conjunction of both liberation and definition provides an excellent recapitulation of the previous section of this chapter ("Autobiography as Repetition"), for the self is both defined and liberated in the act of writing one's life. The perilous journey through time forms the stuff of the autobiographer's story. Without (a revolutionary) awareness of time, Gusdorf and Cox suggest, autobiography would find no place in the literary landscape. Autobiography defines and liberates, yet the very necessity for definition in the wake of liberation is what I find rousing about the study of this field. The obsessive need to define oneself in the modern period points to a dislocation within the very period itself, a period, as Percy

---

42. Gusdorf, "Conditions and Limits," in *Autobiography: Essays,* ed. Olney, 30; Cox, *Recovering Literature's Lost Ground,* 14–15.

sees it, of overwhelming "optimism." If one is not dislocated, if one knows his place in the scheme of things, then there would be no need for self-definition. Yet, as Gusdorf observes, evident at the time is an "impassioned new disquiet."[43]

This period also gave birth to that other problematic literary form—the novel—and it is my contention that the so-called rise of the novel also points to the disquiet, the dislocation of modern man. It is not especially surprising, then, that the insights of both Gusdorf and Cox are remarkably similar to those set forth by Georg Lukács in his *The Theory of the Novel,* for autobiography, like the novel, emerged in response to particular (modern) cultural forces. Lukács' distinction between the epic and novel seems apposite here. The epic represents the endless repetitions of cyclical history, what Kierkegaard might call the recollective posture; time is not problematical because immanence and transcendence have not yet been sundered; travel through time, ostensibly adventurous, is not really so because the traveler through eternally recurring (mythic) time takes no true risks. The novel emerges as a response to the perilous domain of linear, unrepeatable time, wherein immanence and transcendence have been radically sundered ("the novel is the epic of a world that has been abandoned by God"); the life of pure immanence or transcendence and the search for a blending of the two, while adventurous, also become burdensome.[44] The novel, then, as we are often reminded, likewise grapples with the question of time. For it was at the beginning of historical awareness, the beginning of the modern, revolutionary era, that the self proclaimed its independence from traditional and limited definitions, only to find itself displaced and disoriented in time. And it is in this period that the self seeks a sense of stability by means of both the novel and autobiography. The point I wish to make is that questions of the novel, autobiography, and the (modern) self, because of their historical provenance, are inextricably united, and each displays its own version of dislocation or displacement.

I have already mentioned the problems with setting limits to autobiography. The situation with the novel is much the same. Boundaries are obscure, even resisted, as the form reaches now in one direction, now in

43. *Ibid.,* 33.

44. Georg Lukács, *The Theory of the Novel* (Cambridge, Mass., 1971), 88, 30, 56ff.

another. With the coming of the novel, we might say that literature, like the modern self, has been liberated, but in its liberation it has (like the self) both foundered and thrived. It seeks a definition that seems always one step beyond its reach. Walter Reed cogently suggests that the novel is an "outsider" to traditional literary pursuits: "It is this sense of itself as an 'outsider' . . . that I would single out as the most basic feature of the novel as a literary kind. The novel is a deliberate stranger to literary decorum; it insists on placing itself beyond the pale of literary tradition." The novel, liberated sometime during the height of renaissance humanism, cannot define itself within the boundaries of a poetics because it "opposes itself to the view of literature that a poetics implies. Not only does it oppose itself to types of literature more traditional than the novel. . . . A novel characteristically opposes itself to other novels."[45] When the novel makes its appearance on the literary landscape, it destructs, as Spanos might say, the traditional understanding of literature. But, again, this destruction is not a negative phenomenon. Instead, it opens new possibilities, possibilities that were foreclosed in traditional literary production. Just as it was necessary for the "individual qua individual" to come to the fore as a condition for the possibility of autobiography, so, too, in the case of the novel. Ian Watt, for example, says that it was essential for the ordinary activities of ordinary individuals to become notable before the novel could claim attention, a point not significantly different from either Lukács' or Reed's and one remarkably similar to the "conditions" Gusdorf sets forth for autobiography.[46] Furthermore, the novel addresses an audience entirely different from that of traditional literature—the individual. Reed writes: "The audience for these literary fictions is both specific and uncertain. It is not a community of listeners attending to an epic 'song,' or a member of an aristocratic coterie glancing over poems circulated in manuscript. . . . Rather, it is a solitary, anonymous figure, scanning a bulk of printed pages, out of a sense of nothing better to do."[47] The novel addresses Cervantes' "idle reader." And if idleness is the devil's workshop, as the Puritan adage goes, then the displacement of the

45. Reed, *Exemplary History of the Novel*, 3, 7.
46. Ian Watt, *The Rise of the Novel* (Berkeley, 1957), 13ff.
47. Reed, *Exemplary History of the Novel*, 25.

self at the very time the self was being liberated could be considered one aspect of the devil's work.

Now Percy, like Kierkegaard, explores this paradoxical displacement of the self that arrives at the very time the self should be most secure. And like Kierkegaard's objections to the Hegelian system, Percy utters plaintive cries about the regnant world view of our time—modern science. Science, he says, can utter truths about almost every sector of the world, yet "the sector of the world about which science cannot utter a single word is nothing less than this: what it is like to be an individual living in . . . the twentieth century" (*Signposts,* 213). In an interview with Bradley R. Dewey, Percy makes the connection between Hegel and science clear:

> One big difficulty for me in reading Kierkegaard was that I had no philosoph-
> ical training at all, especially about Hegel or the German idealists. That was a
> great obstacle and stumbling block for years. Kierkegaard was attacking Hegel.
> For a long time I thought that was irrelevant. I said, well, what difference does
> it make whether he successfully demolished Hegel or not, until I realized that
> you could very successfully extrapolate his attack on Hegel against what we
> might call scientism. The same thing he said about the Hegelian system might
> be said about a purely scientific view of the world which leaves out the individ-
> ual. So once I made that extrapolation from Hegel, whom I cared nothing
> about, to a whole, scientific, exclusive world view, it became very relevant."
> (*Con,* 117)

The scientist, like the Hegelian philosopher, cannot "utter a single word about an individual thing or creature insofar as it is an individual but only insofar as it resembles other individuals. . . . [Yet] the catch is that each of us is, always and inescapably, an individual" (*Signposts,* 211–12). The diffi-culty of life in the twentieth century, Percy says, derives from a profound transformation of the consciousness of Western man:

> The consciousness of Western man, the layman in particular, has been trans-
> formed by a curious misapprehension of the scientific method. One is tempted
> to use the theological term "idolatry." This misapprehension, which is not the
> fault of science, but rather the inevitable consequence of the victory of the sci-
> entific worldview accompanied as it is by all the dazzling credentials of scientific
> progress [*sic*]. It, the misapprehension, takes the form, I believe, of a radical
> and paradoxical loss of sovereignty by the layman and of a radical impoverish-
> ment of human relations—paradoxical, I say, because it occurs in the very face

of his technological mastery of the world and his richness as a consumer of the world's goods. (*Signposts,* 210)

This loss of sovereignty—this impoverishment—echoes Gusdorf's "impassioned disquiet of modern man," and it points to Percy's view of the novel as diagnostic.

Dislocation and impoverishment occur when the individual chooses to see himself not as "always and inescapably" an individual, but rather from the point of view of science, which cannot say one word about the individual qua individual: "To the degree that we allow ourselves to perceive ourselves as a type of, example of, instance of, such-and-such a class of Homo sapiens—even the most creative Homo sapiens imaginable—to this same degree do we come short of being ourselves" (*Signposts,* 212). There is a "gap," then, in the normative cultural world view. For Percy this gap is best filled by the novelist: "If there is such a gap in the scientific view of the world . . . and if the scientist cannot address himself to this reality . . . [then] the novelist can, and most particularly the novelist" (213). If the previous discussion of autobiography as repetition is accepted, we could say the autobiographer does the same thing. The writing of novels and autobiographies, therefore, takes its place along the side of science as an endeavor that is "cognitive, a kind of finding out and knowing and telling" (207). They both tell of what it is like to be a displaced and dislocated individual in the twentieth century, even when, *especially when,* one does not feel himself to be so dislocated.

But this diagnostic role of the novel is not as new as Percy might lead one to believe. The seeds of the malady Percy diagnoses reside, of course, at the beginning of the modern period—the time of the "scientific revolution." In *The Origins of the English Novel, 1600–1740,* Michael McKeon cites numerous examples of what might be called the "idolatrous" exuberance displayed by some proponents of the new philosophy—*i.e.,* science. The enthusiasm went to such extremes, McKeon observes, that some thought science could offer "solid history" in the place of "romance." As an example McKeon cites Joseph Glanville, who looks forward to the Royal Society's collective and communal efforts to compose histories of nature: "the *Histories of Nature* we have *hitherto* had, have been but an *heap* and *amassment* of *Truth* and *Falsehood, vulgar Tales* and *Romantick* Accounts; and 'tis not in the power of *particular unassociated* Endeavors to afford us better." Ancient systems or endeavors "unassociated" with the new philosophy are considered fabulous "romances," while modern ones are heralded as "solid histories." Yet McKeon points out that the very language used in extolling the endeavors of the Royal Society often mimics that of the romances the Society claims to supersede: "The enthusiasm of Glanville and Thomas Sprat leads both to speak of those 'glorious Undertakers' of the new philosophy as the new, 'illustrious Heroes' of the modern age, greater than those of epic and romance, 'generous Vertuoso's, who dwell in an higher Region then other Mortals.' This heady flirtation with the fanciful idealism of romance seems odd coming from sober empiricists; it expresses the *disorienting* experience of historical relativity with respect both to past dogmas and to future possibilities, which begin now to appear limitless."[48] What McKeon says, it seems to me, is that science, an endeavor that at first appears limitless in its application, carries with it the seeds of its own limitation, disorientation, or dislocation—*the* (post)modern predicament.

But disorientation is but one of the many instabilities that occurred during the time of the "rise" of the novel. McKeon argues that the era exemplifies two broader "instabilities" that include as a facet the one noted above—instabilities with regard to "generic categories" ("questions of truth") and "social categories" ("questions of virtue"). The novel emerges at this time, it gains its own limited stability, "because of its unrivaled power both to formulate, and to explain, a set of problems that are central to early modern experience." McKeon goes so far as to say that the new form triumphs as "an explanatory and problem-solving mode." It tries to answer questions of truth and questions of virtue, and thus provide some stability, some definition, to the liberated self.

McKeon's line of thought, then, is not very different from Percy's. For diagnosis (to "know through or between") is but the attempt to explain and to solve some problem. The time of the rise of the novel is also a time, as McKeon would say, of the "categorical instability" of the self. Notions of self and place in society (questions of truth and virtue) become problematic. Dislocation ensues. Although this dislocation or instability does not attain the severity it achieves in the twentieth century, it, like the novel,

---

48. McKeon, *Origins of the English Novel,* 68, 69 (my emphasis).

displays what McKeon calls a "pregiveness." It does not " 'persist' into the realm of the modern as an alien intrusion from without." Rather, it is akin to what Marx calls a " 'simple abstraction,' a deceptively monolithic category that encloses a complex historical process."[49] Thus, the seeds of the impoverishment of the self, which Percy cites as the problem of life in the twentieth century, the problem that the postmodern novel may diagnose, reside within the era of the origins of the novel. The beginning of the modern age carries the seeds of the postmodern one. In this particular epoch, the liberated self, the outsider, finds itself in the paradoxical situation of seeking definition in the two forms that resist definition, forms that arise to treat the individual as individual rather than as a specimen of the scientific method. The two forms are, of course, the novel and autobiography.

The novel and autobiography serve similar functions, then, and to say that Percy's use of the novel is autobiographical is to say that he uses it to retrieve or repeat possibilities of the self that the normative cultural understanding (enmeshed as it is in scientism) forecloses. It is the individual as individual that Percy tries to retrieve from the deadening effects of an "idolatrous" worship of science. His novels "de-struct" the "deficient polarizations of spirit" that such a worship of science fosters. The self, as Percy sees it, is neither purely transcendent (the recollective posture of science and art) nor purely immanent (a consumer of the world's goods). Neither is it, as he writes in *Love in the Ruins,* a "mythical monster," a strange hybrid of the two in the fashion of Dr. Jekyll and Mr. Hyde (*LR,* 382–83). Instead, the "repeated" self finds itself in the same posture as Spanos' genuine interpreter—that is, a *homo viator,* a wayfarer, pilgrim, or castaway whose feelings of uncanniness and dislocation (*unheimlicheit*) compel him to look for signs of the transcendent in the realm of the immanent, and thereby to redeem his time. In Percy's postmodern world, the road to this redemption becomes clear, paradoxically, only in the aftermath of some sort of violence or situation of ordeal, some "de-struction" of ordinary contexts. Recall the museum episode in *The Last Gentleman.* Will Barrett is able to "see" the paintings only after an accident (a type of destruction or de-structuring of the ordinary museum context) occurs. So lost is the self to itself that it takes such a situation to wrest it from the shackles of complacency, at-homeness,

49. *Ibid.,* 20–21.

and to restore it to its wayfaring state. Percy's linguistic philosophy and a reading of his first two novels in light of that philosophy provide a more practical understanding of repetition and the postmodern predicament of the displaced self. Like autobiography and the novel, Percy's language theory, itself outside the pale of traditional thought on the subject, attempts to retrieve the self to a state of "being between" and thus of being interested in time.

2

Repetition and *Autos:* The Unformulability of the Self

A SEMIOTICS OF THE SELF

While it seems fairly evident that Percy views the novel (and thus autobiography) from a posture of repetition, his study of semiotics offers more fruitful territory for discussing the centrality of that category in his works. What Percy does with the novel, he does also with semiotics. He sunders traditional boundaries set up in professional circles, and from a posture somewhere between professional and amateur, he challenges the discipline to open itself to new possibilities. He "de-structs," that is to say, the closure imposed by "specialization" in "fields of study" with the hope of retrieving possibilities that have been foreclosed or overlooked by conventional methodologies.

In "The Delta Factor," the introductory essay to *The Message in the Bottle,* Percy reflects on the origins of the book: "It is the meager fruit of twenty years' off-and-on thinking about the subject, of coming at it

47

from one direction, followed by failure and depression and giving up, followed by making up novels to raise my spirits, followed by a new try from a different direction or from an old direction but at a different level, followed by failure, followed by making up another novel, and so on" (*MB*, 10). Written in the early 1970s, this comment both catalogs and foreshadows Percy's continuing interest in semiotics. In 1983, with the publication of *Lost in the Cosmos,* after completing *Lancelot* and *The Second Coming,* Percy returned to what he once referred to as his "extra-literary pursuit," semiotics.[1] And his final letter to Shelby Foote indicates that after the publication of *The Thanatos Syndrome* in 1987, Percy had once again returned to his favorite avocation. After some sobering reflections on his terminal illness and his "search for a cure," Percy writes: "Like I say, it's too damn much trouble, this running around looking for a cure. I'm content to sit here and try to finish *Contra Gentiles,* a somewhat smart-ass collection of occasional pieces, including one which should interest you—'Three New Signs, All More Important than and Different from the 59,018 Signs of Charles Sanders Peirce'—you want a copy?" Foote could never understand Percy's interest in linguistic philosophy. He wrote a letter to Percy on July 10, 1953, not long before Percy was to publish his first philosophical essay, "Symbol as Need." He writes: "I of course know nothing of Symbolic Forms. Go your way. But it seems to me that any philosophy that tries to co-relate [*sic*] (if that means unify in any sense) Art, Religion, Language, etc., is bound to wind up an unholy mess—most especially if psychiatry is included, which doesn't match with anything but logic and even perverts that sophistically to its uses."[2]

Percy's interest in semiotics, then, spans the thirty-six years of his writing career. The cycle—study of language, novel, back to language study—while not entirely consistent, nevertheless points to a "methodology of repetition." What Percy tries to do time and again in his writings on semiotics is to "sketch the beginnings of a theory of man" for an age that has no such

---

1. The quotation is taken from a letter Percy wrote to Lewis Simpson and that Simpson used in the as yet unpublished "Walker Percy's Vision of the Modern World," the Flora Levy Lecture in the Humanities, March 7, 1991, University of Southwestern Louisiana.

2. Walker Percy to Shelby Foote, July 29, 1989, in Walker Percy Papers, #4294, SHC; Shelby Foote to Walker Percy, July 10, 1953, in Shelby Foote Papers, #4038, SHC.

consensus theory (*MB,* 10). He agrees with Alexander Pope who said that "the proper study of man is man" (*MB,* 10), but he focuses his attention on that unique characteristic of human beings, their ability to utter words and sentences and have them understood or misunderstood by another person. Percy looks for a link between language use and an understanding of the self. Thus, he subtitles *The Message in the Bottle: How Queer Man Is, How Queer Language Is, and What One Has to Do with the Other.*

Percy is not interested so much in the formal aspects of language. Neither is he concerned primarily with the mechanics of linguistic transactions. Rather, he struggles to understand sign users by means of their sign-using activity: "the book is not about language but about the creatures who use it and what happens when they do" (*MB,* 11). In itself this step is a retrieval of a possibility that the tradition has not explored. As Percy sees it, the two broad traditions that have grappled with a theory of language—the behavioral and the formal—miss the phenomenon itself: "American behaviorists kept solid hold on the world of things and creatures, yet couldn't fit the symbol into it. German idealists kept the word as internal form, logos, and let the world get away" (*MB,* 33).

These traditions, as venerable as they are, can nevertheless be viewed as "deficient polarizations" of the phenomenon. On the one hand, behaviorists place man as an organism in an environment. Like other animals, we have needs that can be fulfilled by the manipulation of our surroundings—hence, the proliferation of countless items and techniques manufactured to help us "adjust." Homeostasis is the goal. Yet this same tradition cannot account for the very behaviorists who write down theories and submit articles with the expectation that they will be read and understood. The behaviorists write from a posture of *aeterno modo*—a recollective stance that transcends time. The stimulus-response model, no matter how complicated, cannot account for the *meaning* that exchanges between a reader and a writer, an utterer and an interpretant, even if what is written or uttered is misunderstood or misinterpreted. According to Percy, then, the behaviorist remains outside of his own theory.

The formalists or idealists, on the other hand, place man within the confines of his own mind, within the cell of himself, radically disconnected from both the world and others, unable to enter the "ordinary lovely world." While this tradition offers sound theories regarding the building blocks of language, such an abstracted posture nevertheless ends in solipsism. The self is stranded within itself, cut off from the very meanings its mind generates.

Percy's methodology of repetition seeks a third way, not through a Hegelian, world-historical synthesis of opposites, which, of course, falls into the latter polarization, but from an observation of the phenomenon itself: "Instead of marking [man] down at the outset as besouled creature or responding organism, why not look at him as he appears, not even as *Homo sapiens,* because attributing sapience already begs the question, but as *Homo loquens,* man the talker, or *Homo symbolificus,* man the symbol-monger?" (*MB,* 17). Percy's interest in semiotics turns to the symbol user himself—a retrieval of a possibility that has been overlooked in the tradition. By way of parenthesis, it is interesting to note that in *Bright Air, Brilliant Fire: On the Matter of the Mind,* Gerald M. Edelman attempts something akin to Percy but from a biological and neuro-anatomical framework. Edelman's comments on language sound remarkably similar to Percy's.[3]

In *Lost in the Cosmos,* Percy again comes at the issue "from a different level." The "warning-challenge-announcement-introduction" to the Intermezzo section suggests the retrieval Percy is about to undertake: "[This section] will irritate many professional semioticists by not being technical enough—and for focusing on one dimension of semiotics which semioticists, for whatever reason, are not accustomed to regard as a proper subject of inquiry, *i.e.,* not texts and other coded sign utterances but the self which produces texts or hears sign utterances" (*LC,* 83). The Intermezzo can also be seen as Percy's synthesis of his thirty years' interest in the field, a synopsis of the essays collected in *The Message in the Bottle.* As such, it is his clearest statement of his approach to semiotics—*i.e.,* a semiotics of the self, hence the title, "A Semiotic Primer of the Self." His own comments point to the centrality it has with respect to his work as a whole: "Despite its offhand tone, [the 'Primer' is] as serious as can be. I have never [done] and will never do anything as important. If I am remembered for anything a hundred years from now, it will probably be for that" (*Con,* 285).

At this point it also becomes necessary to regularize my use of terms.

---

3. Gerald M. Edelman, *Bright Air, Brilliant Fire: On the Matter of the Mind* (New York, 1992).

In his earlier writings Percy followed Susanne Langer's and Peirce's distinction between sign and symbol: "Signs announce their objects. Thunder announces rain. The bell announces food to Pavlov's dog. When I say James to a dog, he *looks* for James; when I say James to you, you say, "What about him?"—you *think* about James. A symbol is the vehicle for the conception of an object and as such is a distinctively human product" (*MB,* 293). Peirce used "sign" to denote the dyadic behavior of organisms and "symbol" to denote the triadic behavior of humans (see *LC,* 87, note). In his later writings, however, Percy adopted De Saussure's use of "signal" to denote that which announces its object and "sign" to denote the vehicle for the conception of an object. I will follow Percy's later usage from here on.

Not all critics share Percy's enthusiasm about the Intermezzo section of *Lost in the Cosmos.* In *The Fiction of Walker Percy,* John Edward Hardy, for one, writes that he "cannot agree" with Percy's own assessment of the piece: "I imagine that Percy would have had difficulty in finding a publisher even for an essay collection like *The Message in the Bottle,* not to speak of *Lost in the Cosmos,* if he had not established a reputation as a novelist. . . . His greater talent is for fiction."[4] Hardy's point rings true. Yet it may apply more readily to *Lost in the Cosmos* than to *The Message in the Bottle.* While there may have been no cause for a *collection* of such essays (in *Message*) had Percy not been a fiction writer, it is important to remember that these essays gained placement in respectable scholarly journals on their own strengths. Thus, they were recognized as having something important to add to the study of language and the language user regardless of Percy's fiction writing. Percy's enthusiasm for "A Semiotic Primer of the Self" reflects, I think, his awareness of the synthesis he had wrought, of his having brought together his many years' thoughts on the subject concisely, coherently, and humorously. It is noteworthy, furthermore, that the manuscript material surrounding *Lost in the Cosmos* begins with material that eventually finds its way into this Intermezzo section, suggesting, as does its final placement in the published edition, its centrality. Although I am in no position to forecast Percy's reception one hundred years from now, I am more inclined than Hardy to accept his own excitement about this work.

The subtitle of the "Primer," while jocular in tone, further points to its

---

4. John Edward Hardy, *The Fiction of Walker Percy* (Urbana, 1987), 19.

character of retrieval: "A Short History of the Cosmos with Emphasis on the Nature and Origin of the Self, Plus a Semiotic Model for Computing Impoverishment in the Midst of Plenty, or Why It is Possible to Feel Bad in a Good Environment and Good in a Bad Environment" (*LC*, 85). Percy reintroduces concerns that have been with him from his earliest days of publishing, but comes at the subject here in terms of a "History of the Cosmos." And the latter part of the title not only echoes the long set of questions that begin "The Delta Factor," but also suggests one of Percy's central themes. Why do his characters feel so bad when they have the best of possible surroundings? Percy's attempt to work out this problem "semiotically" suggests that his fiction and nonfiction are also of a piece. While both can stand autonomously, they are nevertheless complementary.

This blending of the two dimensions of Percy's work is not new. Almost every writer who has grappled with Percy's fiction has had recourse to his nonfiction. Hardy is a notable exception, although he refers to Percy's linguistic pieces from time to time. I do not wholly agree with Hardy when he says that Percy's "own comments [in his nonfiction pieces and interviews] do not form a coherent system for critical interpretation and evaluation of any works of fiction, his own notably included." Percy's methodology in both his fiction and nonfiction, as I hope to show, reflects his attempt at repetition or retrieval, and thus makes his work "all of a piece." Lewis Lawson seems to maintain the same thing in his review of Hardy's work.[5]

In the "Primer," Percy retrieves from the tradition of linguistic study the work of Charles Sanders Peirce. Just as Heidegger turned to the meditations of Descartes as he struggled to renew the question of being, so Percy turns to Peirce for help with his semiotics. Of course, Percy uses Peirce throughout his writings on language, not only at the time of writing *Lost in the Cosmos*. He was aware all along that he was building his own thoughts on Peirce's shoulders. On February 3, 1971, he wrote to Foote about his language philosophy: "I would even say that it is revolutionary: that one hundred years from now it could well be known as the Peirce-Percy theory of meaning (not Pierce but Peirce and so pronounced Perce-Percy)." Peir-

5. Hardy, *The Fiction of Walker Percy*, 19; Lewis A. Lawson, "Hardy Thinking on Percy," *Southern Literary Journal*, XXI (1989), 113–18.

ce's presence, however, seems to be stronger in *Cosmos* because the "Primer" begins with Peirce's distinction between dyadic and triadic interactions.[6]

For Percy, the cosmos has manifested a predominance of dyadic events. His history, then, begins with an explanation of what they are: "From the beginning and for most of the fifteen billion years of the life of the Cosmos, there was only one kind of event. It was particles hitting particles, chemical reactions, energy exchanges, gravity attractions between masses, field forces, and so on. As different as such events are, they can be understood as an interaction between two or more entities: $A \rightleftarrows B$. Even a system as inconceivably vast as the Cosmos itself can be understood as such an interaction" (*LC*, 85–86). With the appearance of organic life "some three and a half billion years ago," interactions both within a single organism and between two or more organisms could still be understood dyadically (*LC*, 88). Organisms inhabit an environment, to which they respond in order to maintain an inner balance, homeostasis. An organism's response to its environment and to other organisms can be understood as a signal response, that is to say, dyadic. Since signals announce their objects, such signal responses might include the response to flee, the call to mate, or, as in the case of ants and bees, directions toward food. No matter how complex, and no matter how many variables involved, such interactions can still be expressed by the formula $A \rightleftarrows B$.

Triadic behavior, on the other hand, did not enter the cosmos until very recently, "perhaps less than 100,000 years ago, perhaps more." It is an event "different in kind from all preceding events in the Cosmos. It cannot be understood as a dyadic interaction or a complexus of dyadic interactions. . . . It is that event in which sign *A* is understood by organism *B*, not as a signal to flee or approach, but as 'meaning' or referring to another perceived segment of the environment" (*LC*, 95–96).

Percy views Helen Keller's experience at the well house with Anne Sullivan as the paradigmatic triadic episode.[7] Before the well-house event,

---

6. Walker Percy to Shelby Foote, February 3, 1971, in Percy Papers, SHC; for a good overview of Percy's relation to Peirce, see J. P. Tellote, "Charles Peirce and Walker Percy: From Semiotic to Narrative," *Southern Quarterly*, XVIII (1980), 65–79.

7. Helen Keller, *The Story of My Life* (New York, 1954). Percy refers to Keller's acquisition of language repeatedly in his essays, not just here.

Keller responded to Sullivan's words (spelled in her hand) as signals. But when Sullivan put one of Keller's hands underneath the water flowing out of the well and in her other hand spelled out w-a-t-e-r, Keller was quite literally born into the world of triadic behavior. She realized that the word was somehow connected to the thing, that it "meant" the cool liquid flowing over her hand. The connection between the word spelled, the actual thing, and Helen Keller herself form the angles of an irreducible triangle—hence, triadic behavior, or what Percy calls the "Delta Factor," the Greek letter (Δ) a symbol for irreducibility. For Percy the three relations—between Keller and the word, Keller and the actual water, and the word and the thing—cannot be explained dyadically. This event marks Keller's crossing over the threshold of sign use. No longer do Sullivan's words announce something to Keller; no longer are they signals. Instead, she has entered the realm of the triad—of meaning. Although she is still an organism in an environment with needs to be fulfilled, Percy emphasizes that her newfound sign use *places* her also in a *world*. In words remarkably similar to Percy's, Gerald M. Edelman says the following: "Once a self is developed through social and linguistic interactions on a base of primary consciousness, a world is developed that *requires* naming and intending. This world reflects inner events that are recalled, and imagined events, as well as outside events that are perceptually experienced. Tragedy becomes possible—the loss of the self by death or mental disorder, the remembrance of unassuageable pain. By the same token, a high drama of creation and endless imagination emerges."[8]

This idea of placement in a world is central to an understanding of Percy's semiotics of self, and it parallels Janet Varner Gunn's writings on autobiography (discussed in Chapter 1), which also concern the self's primary confrontation with place—"Where am I?" For Gunn, as for Percy, the self's placement is problematic, else why ask the question in the first place. Autobiography and Percy's works as autobiography attempt to name the self's predicament in relation to place (and thus also to time). I will return to this notion shortly. For now, however, I wish to address Percy's use of *sign*. I have already noted that Percy follows De Saussure in his later writings and uses *signal* and *sign* (as opposed to *sign* and *symbol* in his earlier

8. Edelman, *Bright Air,* 136.

writings) for the difference between announcement and conception. Yet when he begins to discuss triadic behavior and sign use on page 95 of the "Primer," he seems to put De Saussure's distinction between *signifiant* (signifier) and *signifié* (signified) to his own use. For Percy the former is the word itself and the latter is the referent or thing. But this is not De Saussure's meaning of the terms. It is not until page 102 that Percy acknowledges De Saussure's use of the two terms: "The sign, as Saussure said, is a union of signifier (the sound-image of a word) and signified (the concept of an object, action, quality)." Then he adds in a footnote that the *signifié* is neither a percept nor a concept, but something in between, a " 'concrete concept' or an 'abstract percept,' or what Gerard Manley Hopkins called *inscape*." For Percy, then, the conjunction of the signifier and the signified, in its paradigmatic or primordial form, places an object, action, or quality somewhere between the concrete and the abstract: "What comes to mind when I hear *apple,* what in fact the word articulates within itself, is neither an individual apple [percept] nor a definition of *apple* [concept], but a quality of appleness . . ." (*LC,* 102, note).

Despite his somewhat equivocal use of De Saussure, Percy places his thought precisely where he wants it to be. The sign exemplifies a state of being between (*inter esse*). From Percy's own standpoint between the behaviorists (for whom everything exists in the realm of the concrete) and the idealists or formalists (for whom the abstract holds priority), the sign exhibits its own *inter esse*. Thus, sign use, in its primordial form, enacts a repetition for sign users. It places them in a relation of interest—in the double sense of "being between" and "concerned." The paradigmatic sign-using event is itself a repetition.[9]

---

9. Helen Keller's description of the well-house episode is worth recounting in its entirety, as Percy does in "The Delta Factor" (*MB,* 35), for even her diction points to the repetition that she has experienced:

We walked down the path to the well-house, attracted by the fragrance of the honeysuckle with which it was covered. Someone was drawing water and my teacher placed my hand under the spout. As the cool stream gushed over one hand, she spelled into the other the word *water,* first slowly then rapidly. I stood still, my whole attention fixed upon the motion of her fingers. Suddenly I felt a misty consciousness as of something forgotten—a thrill of returning thought; and somehow the mystery of language was revealed to me. I knew then that "w-a-t-e-r" meant the wonderful cool something that was flowing over my hand. That living word

Every act of naming, the "Primer" continues, involves both a namer and a receiver of the name. The irreducible triad really involves two triangles—one for the sign utterer and one for the sign receiver: "Every triad of sign-reception requires another triad of sign-utterance. Whether the sign is a word, a painting, or a symphony—or Robinson Crusoe writing a journal to himself—a sign transaction requires a sign-utterer and a sign-receiver" (*LC*, 96). Anne Sullivan is not merely an ancillary participant in Helen Keller's breakthrough to triadicity. For Percy she relates as an inter-subjective "co-celebrant" to the being that primordial sign use names. A child learning to name things stands in the same repetitive posture as Helen Keller. Sign use is social in origin, an "intersubjective" event.[10]

As a result of this social nature, Percy offers a fresh view of consciousness. In its etymological sense, *conscious* means "to know with." For Percy this "knowing with" carries a double reference—to the sign with which we "know" a thing, and to the other (the namer or the receiver of the name) with whom we know it. Thus, the Cartesian or Husserlian formula for consciousness—"I am conscious of this chair"—and the Sartrean revision of it—"There is consciousness of this chair"—can be further revised as "This 'is' a chair for you and me" (See *MB*, 275–76). For Percy sign use constitutes consciousness. Since "one is always conscious *of* something *as* something—its sign—[then] it is part of the act of consciousness to *place* [that

---

awakened my soul, gave it light, hope, joy, set it free! There were barriers still, it is true, but barriers that could in time be swept away.

I left the well-house eager to learn. Everything had a name, and each name gave birth to a new thought. As we returned to the house every object which I touched seemed to quiver with life. That was because I saw everything with the strange, new sight that had come to me. On entering the door I remembered the doll I had broken. [She had earlier destroyed the doll in a fit of temper.] I felt my way to the hearth and picked up the pieces. I tried vainly to put them together. Then my eyes filled with tears; for I realized what I had done, and for the first time I felt repentance and sorrow.

I learned a great many new words that day. I do not remember what they all were; but I do know that *mother, father, sister, teacher* were among them—words that were to make the world blossom for me, "like Aaron's rod with flowers." It would have been difficult to find a happier child than I was as I lay in my crib at the close of that eventful day and lived over the joys it had brought me, and for the first time longed for a new day to come.

10. See Mary Deems Howland, *The Gift of the Other: Gabriel Marcel's Concept of Intersubjectivity in Walker Percy's Novels* (Pittsburgh, 1990).

something].... The signing process tends to configure segments of the Cosmos under the auspices of a sign, often mistakenly" (*LC,* 106). A particular interplay of light and shade may *look* like a rabbit, but upon closer inspection turn out to be only the shadow of a bush. Furthermore, entities denoted by such names as "unicorn" and "the boogerman" may find a place in the *world* of the triadic sign user even though they have no corresponding physical existence. The sign user inhabits and designates a world.

It is interesting to note that, unlike the placing that occurs in the act of consciousness for Percy, Sartre depicts Roquentin's paradigmatic experience of consciousness in *La Nausée* as a cutting loose of the world in all its viscosity. Percy himself says that one of the central scenes in *The Last Gentleman,* to be explored later in this chapter, "was written as a kind of counterstatement" to Sartre's novel.[11]

But the Edenic, paradigmatic sign-using event of Helen Keller at the well house, or of a child learning to name, harbors a two-headed snake in the grass. On the one hand, the signifier is "interpenetrated" by the signified to the degree that a devaluation occurs. No longer does the signifier reveal the signified, but rather it seals it off. There takes place "a hardening and a closure of the signifier, so that in the end the signified becomes encased in a simulacrum like a mummy in a mummy case" (*LC,* 104). On the other hand, while the act of consciousness places things in the world by means of signs, there is no sign that can encompass the sign user himself: "The fateful flaw of human semiotics is this: that of all the objects in the entire Cosmos which the sign-user can apprehend through the conjoining of signifier and signified (word uttered and thing beheld), there is one which forever escapes his comprehension—and that is the sign-user himself. Semiotically, the self is literally unspeakable to itself.... The self has no sign of itself. No signifier applies. All signifiers apply equally."[12] The self, then, cannot be placed in the act of consciousness, even though it is conscious of itself. From the aspect of semiotics, then, the self is dislocated. Gerald Edelman,

---

11. *Signposts,* 221. See also Spanos, *Repetitions,* Chapter 2, "The Un-naming of the Beasts: The Postmodernity of Sartre's *La Nausée.*"

12. *LC,* 106–107. Percy repeats this insight in different ways in *MB,* see especially pages 9 and 283. In this context the "I" for Percy would seem to correspond to what Emile Benveniste has called an "empty signifier," one whose designation changes with each use. See Emile Benveniste, *Problems in General Linguistics* (Coral Gables, Fla., 1973), 218ff.

again, corroborates Percy's fundamental insight: "Ironically, the self is the last thing to be understood by its possessor, even after the possession of a theory of consciousness."[13] Percy seems to go further than Edelman, however, in his assertion that the self is quite literally adrift and not merely "the last thing to be understood." Percy argues that the self, bereft of a consensus theory of the kind that informed Europe in the twelfth century or New England in the seventeenth, literally has no place in the cosmos. It is unformulable, "lost in the cosmos," forever seeking its place. "Where am I?" becomes the postmodern, autobiographical question. Percy's works, like autobiography, explore this question.

It may be useful to take this unformulability of the self as an analogue of the "dread that has no object" discussed in Chapter 1. The transformation of dread into fear (the objectification of dread) bears a striking resemblance to the self seeking placement in the world. Placement is the key, but when the traditional modes of placement—Totemism, Eastern Pantheism, and Judeo-Christianity—are declared inadmissible by the postmodern world, the self is left with only two options—immanence or transcendence. In such a world, the self seeks to quell the dread of nonplacement by objectifying itself. It seeks a sign. In our postreligious and postmythic age, the self seeks its sign either by taking its place as an immanent consumer of the goods that a scientific and technological culture provides for it—*i.e.,* allowing goods and techniques to give it form—or by adopting the objective posture of science itself—*i.e.,* transcending the world so as to make pronouncements about it.

Art offers another means of transcendence. The difference, however, between the transcendence of science and that of art is that whereas the scientist speaks to a relatively small transcendent community of scientists, the artist speaks "to the world of men who understand him" (*LC,* 119). The artist names the unnameable and forms the unformulable. For an age in which the self finds no sign for itself, the artist provides the service of at least naming this predicament: "If Kafka's *Metamorphosis* is presently a more accurate account of the self than Beethoven's Ninth Symphony, it is the more exhilarating for being so. The naming of the predicament of the self by art is its reversal. Hence the salvific effect of art. Through art, the predic-

13. Edelman, *Bright Air,* 136.

ament of self becomes not only speakable but laughable. . . . Kafka and his friends laughed when he read his stories to them" (*LC,* 121). But the transcendence that art provides is more ephemeral than that of science. The artist's placement is more tenuous.

Scientists can remain "in orbit" as long as the community of fellow Olympians accepts their dicta. They have relatively few problems leaving orbit to "reenter" momentarily the world. The artist participates in community at the time of creating his art, yet he suffers "spectacular reentries and flameouts" when he finishes his work and tries to reenter the ordinary world. These attempts at reentry bear witness to "nothing other than a pathology of the self in the twentieth century" (*LC,* 122), one of Percy's ultimate concerns as a writer.

The question of placement in the world was a personal one for Percy. In his funny "Why I Live Where I Live," he addresses it in relation to his adopted hometown of Covington, Louisiana, which he calls a "pleasant nonplace," somewhere between the placement of New Orleans and the displacement of Europe or the Caribbean. Patrick Samway, S.J., has shown, furthermore, how Percy's fiction finds its way ultimately to this "nonplace" in his novels—especially in *The Thanatos Syndrome,* which takes place in a town something like Covington and something like St. Francisville, Louisiana, an area where some of the earliest Percys settled—as though the novelist were drawn to, although not quite at home with, his ancestral soil.[14]

It is also interesting to note that in his reflections on writers, Percy cites Faulkner's drinking and Hemingway's travels as indicative of the dislocations and the problems of reentry that artists suffer (*LC,* 123, 141ff.). He marvels time and again at Eudora Welty's ability to live an ordinary life in her childhood home, apparently without the symptoms or the problems of reentry that her male counterparts face (see *MCon,* 29, and *LC,* 147). There is a sense, then, in which Percy's portrayal of the self might be seen as "gen-

---

14. Patrick H. Samway, S.J., "A Writer at Home in Louisiana," in *Cross, Crosier, and Crucible: A Volume Celebrating the Bicentennial of a Catholic Diocese in Louisiana (1793–1993),* ed. Glenn R. Conrad (Lafayette, La., 1993). For more on Percy and place see John Edward Hardy, "Percy and Place: Some Beginnings and Endings," *Southern Quarterly,* XVIII (1980), 5–25; Richard Pindell, "Toward Home: Place, Language, and Death in *The Last Gentleman,*" in *The Art of Walker Percy: Stratagems for Being,* ed. Panthea Reid Broughton, 50–68. See also Wyatt-Brown, *House of Percy,* 334–55.

dered." It is predominantly men who suffer the radical bifurcation of immanence and transcendence and who are most in need of "reentry" and most in danger of "flameouts."

His fiction seems to bear out this point. It is largely the male characters who suffer bouts of angelism/bestialism. The female characters are, to paraphrase Sheila Bosworth, "something to wonder at." They help the male protagonists find their way back to the ordinary world.[15] It is also true that many of Percy's female characters serve as doubles of his protagonists and thus evince another level of repetition. In *The Moviegoer,* Kate tells Binx: "You're like me, but worse. Much worse" (*MG,* 43). Will Barrett sees himself in Kitty Vaught (*LG,* 8). In *Love in the Ruins* Tom More—who suffers most profoundly from the very syndrome he has named, More's Syndrome, or chronic angelism/bestialism—seems to have three doubles, each representative of a dimension of himself. Will and Allie form ideal complements for one another in *The Second Coming.* Despite this doubling, however, the male perspective dominates almost exclusively. Percy's stories concern men who find themselves abstracted and dislocated and then look for options of reentry. A notable exception arises in the character of Allie, whom Percy himself called "one of the few women characters [he's] been pleased with" (*Con,* 229). Although a third-person narrative like the rest of *The Second Coming,* her story marks a departure from Percy's usual narrative perspective.

There is a sense, too, in which the transcendence/immanence continuum divides along gender lines. Male characters, especially the central ones, are more likely to display problems of transcendence (and subsequent reentry difficulties), whereas females seem sunk more in everyday concerns, the sphere of immanence. Although Allie has suffered bouts of abstraction, her story deals primarily with the struggle to build a home for herself, wonderfully evoked by the reconstruction of the stove. Thus, for most of the novel she remains in the immanent sphere, in the world of blocks, tackles, and hoists. Will, on the other hand, lost in the realm of transcendence, needs someone to shoot at him before he recovers any sense of the imma-

---

15. Sheila Bosworth, "Women in the Fiction of Walker Percy," paper delivered at the 1993 Walker Percy Symposium, March 20, 1993, sponsored by the St. Tammany Parish Library.

nent. Josephine Humphries, whose writing, Fred Hobson points out, follows in the tradition of Percy, seems to have absorbed this same split.[16] In *Dreams of Sleep,* for example, Alice (another Allie?), who was once a mathematician, seems sunk in, almost smothered by, the world of domesticity and immanence. She longs for some outlet. Will (another Will!), on the other hand, suffers symptoms of too much transcendence. Much like Will and Allie of *The Second Coming,* Humphries' characters try to come together again and so reunite immanence and transcendence.

Some exceptions to this division of the continuum do exist. In *The Last Gentleman,* Rita displays characteristics of a self lost in the abstractions of scientific humanism, as does Moira in *Love in the Ruins.* And since Kate serves as a female double to Binx, she also suffers from too much transcendence. Percy's point is that given the self's (male or female) unformulability, immanence and transcendence remain the only options for getting along in the world. That he writes predominantly from the male (abstracted) perspective suggests that he is writing from what he knows best. He once told an interviewer that because he grew up in a male household with Uncle Will and his brothers, he pleads "ignorance" on women.[17]

Questions of the gendered self aside, Percy's notion of the transcendence of art sounds suspiciously modernist. Is he a closet modernist hiding in postmodern garb? When he writes about art providing an avenue of transcendence and about its salvific effect, he sounds similar to that high modernist James Joyce, whose Stephen Dedalus reveled in "epiphanic moments of transcendence" and who liked to speak of salvation by art. Is Percy inconsistent?

If art is a sign that names the unnameable for its age, and if a sign is, as we have seen, somewhere between the abstraction and generality of a concept and the concreteness and individuality of a percept, then for Percy art cannot wholly exemplify the type of transcendence of which Stephen Dedalus speaks. Abstraction and generality belong to the category of transcendence, since what they propose is definition or classification. Concrete-

16. Fred Hobson, *The Southern Writer in the Postmodern World* (Athens, 1991), 58ff.; see also Josephine Humphries, *Dreams of Sleep* (New York, 1984).

17. *Con,* 212. Jay Tolson suggests the problem may be more repression than ignorance. See *Pilgrim in the Ruins,* Introduction.

ness and individuality, on the other hand, fall into the category of immanence. If art provides a sign for the self in an age wherein the self has no
sign, then the sign itself must partake of both immanence and transcendence, thus enacting the repetition outlined in Chapter 1. Furthermore, if a
poet can "wrench [a] signifier out of context and exhibit it in all its queerness" (*LC,* 105), thus forestalling the interpenetration of the signifier by the
signified, then art as a sign should resist this same interpenetration and so
withstand the closure into form that Percy seems to be espousing here by
what could be taken as his tacit modernism, a Joycean, "transcendental"
view.

In other words, if the self is unformulable, then the naming of this
unformulability in a work of art, because the naming is itself a sign, cannot
close the gap between the signifier and the signified. It is the nature of the
sign to "devolve," for the signifier and the signified to interpenetrate. Yet it
is the nature of art to counteract this interpenetration, to establish once
again a distance between the two elements of the sign. As a sign itself, art
endeavors to restore the sign to its rightful posture. The sign that art provides subverts the devolution of the sign by restoring what Samuel Pickering might call "the right distance" between the signifier and the signified.[18]
In this space of the naming act, the self finds its transcendence, not as a
Joycean abandonment of immanence, nor as a conflation of immanence and
transcendence, but somewhere between the two—*inter esse.* For Percy art
enacts its "reversal" in the space of the naming act itself. Joyce's "salvific"
art returns to a time outside time—the mythic *illud tempus.* But Percy's
naming function of art repeats or retrieves the present time in interest—*now*
is the time. What has been, to paraphrase Kierkegaard, now becomes. Joyce's Daedelus recollects the Great Moment of myth, but Percy's naming
makes possible the present. The self seeks its place, not in the mythic age of
beginnings, but now. The unformulable self, then, can be restored to its
posture of interest in the act of naming this same unformulability. Distance
and difference are the keys.

In one of his interviews, Percy discusses this very issue of a gap or
distance. Referring once again to the Helen Keller episode, he says: "But

18. Samuel F. Pickering, Jr. "The Right Distance," in *The Right Distance* (Athens, 1987),
11–18.

the two couldn't be more different; I mean the symbol water couldn't be more different—whether spoken or spelled into her hand—than the liquid flowing over her other hand. So you can hear her saying it, but there has to be a space, separation, or difference between the symbol and the thing in order for the thing to be grasped" (*Con,* 227). And in this same interview, when asked whether he agreed with Dedalus' salvific view of art and language, Percy responded: "No, unfortunately I'm much more pessimistic; I would see Kierkegaard as a good corrective of that. I could imagine Kierkegaard seeing—had he lived after Joyce—seeing Joyce as what he would call a hero of the aesthetic, seeing salvation through art and language. What is that great phrase that Stephen Dedalus uses in one place: 'forge in the smithy of my soul the uncreated conscience of my race.' Kierkegaard would say that's the aesthetic sphere" (*Con,* 231).

What might appear as a relapse into modernist thinking, then, really finds its place in postmodernism. In his letters to Foote, Percy often struggled against the "art for art's sake" view that Foote often advocated.[19] And like so much postmodern theory, Percy, too, emphasizes distance and difference. Yet while he argues for the necessity of a gap between the signifier and the signified, he does not suggest their complete rupture, as postmodern theory presupposes. The name is still connected to the thing for Percy, although a space is needed for the name to disclose the thing and for the thing to find formulation in the name. Art names, and what Percy's art and autobiography share is the attempt to name the self.

Like Kierkegaard, Percy tries to point to the existential by means of the aesthetic. Thus, his novels do not provide a Joycean "moment of transcendence" as he seems to suggest toward the end of the "Primer." The form or the name that Percy offers to the unformulable self cannot place a self that is fundamentally dislocated. Percy's comments in the interview and his repeated references to the unformulability of the self in both the "Primer" and in essays from *The Message in the Bottle* suggest that the gap between the signifier and the signified must remain so that the self will not flee the dread of its unformulability and objectify itself. The only name that can place the self in this age—*homo viator*—places it paradoxically "nowhere," between

19. See, for example, Shelby Foote to Walker Percy, November 8, 1951, in Foote Papers, SHC.

the transcendence of art and science and the immanence of consumerism. From this interesting place, the signless *autos* retrieves possibilities in the hope of beginning again in the openness of repetition, in the space of the sign itself. It is no accident that *Lost in the Cosmos* ends with the words: "Do you read me? Come back. Repeat. Come back. Come back. Come back" (262). Repetition involves this "coming back." It is the postmodern movement of the retrieval of the self in time, not the entry of the self to a time outside time and place. Repetition marks the entry of the self into its own time, the *now* that has always been a potentiality but that now becomes. Percy's works ask readers to come back to themselves in time.

THE OPENNESS OF THE SIGN: BINX BOLLING

This section and the one that follows provide some needed grounding for what has been handled up to this point on a highly abstract and analytical level. Two dimensions of the relation between repetition and the unformulability of the self—the openness of the sign and placement in consciousness—lend themselves especially well to a reading of Percy's first two novels: *The Moviegoer* and *The Last Gentleman*.

By now Binx Bolling must be as familiar to readers of American literature as Quentin Compson. While this bemused, ironic, and detached son of the 1950s South tells his story in a subdued, laconic fashion, he nevertheless embodies, like the younger Compson scion, the spirit of his age. If Quentin bears witness to the decline of the rural, aristocratic, and stoic South, then Binx gives shape to the "malaise" that has struck the suburban, homogenized, consumer South. If Quentin succumbs to his disorientation, Binx explores his. Percy once told an interviewer that he viewed Binx as a "Quentin Compson who didn't commit suicide" (*Con,* 300). Thus, as Quentin wallows in his "love of death," Binx examines the death-in-life of a new age. And as the river closes over Quentin's head, Binx looks for signs of a new possibility.

Yet like his creator, Binx eludes any facile designation. At once urbane, charming, and calculating, he senses that something has gone wrong. Even that knowledge, however, does little to inhibit his various stage impersonations. Time and again he tries to objectify his unformulable self. Sometimes he takes the role of a consumer: "I subscribe to *Consumer Reports* and

as a consequence I own a first-class television set, an all but silent air con-
ditioner and a very long lasting deodorant. My armpits never stink" (*MG*,
7). At other times, he plays a scientist: "Until recent years, I read only 'fundamental' books, that is, key books on key subjects, such as *War and Peace*,
the novel of novels; *A Study of History*, a solution to the problem of time;
Schroedinger's *What is Life?*, Einstein's *The Universe as I See It*, and such.
During those years, I stood outside the universe and sought to understand
it" (69). When he plays neither consumer nor scientist, Binx invokes or
emulates the stars of the silver screen: "Ah, William Holden, we already
need you again. Already the fabric is wearing thin without you" (18).

Yet Binx knows that such objectification of his dread cannot satisfy his
"search." His ironic tone subverts the closure he would provide himself in
such playacting and opens him to his own despair. Even the titles of the
books he reads, set in the context of his scientific, "vertical" search, under-
cut the possibility he seeks. How could time be problematic, for example,
if one has read a "solution to the problem of time"? For readers, Binx presents an exfoliation of quandaries. How can they grip someone who has no
grip on himself? How can they trust a narrator who ironizes the keen eye
with which he sizes up his world? How can they follow, in short, a lost
narrator?[20]

John Edward Hardy has argued that *The Moviegoer* suffers as a work of
fiction because "the reader is very often left to labor over gaps that he cannot be confident the author has recognized as such." In a structural analysis
comparing the novel to a segment that appeared as a short story, "Carnival
in Gentilly," Patrick Samway, S.J., suggests, on the other hand, that "the
gaps . . . become pauses between elements of the code, the moments of
silence that make music possible." Samway further suggests that because
The Moviegoer and "Carnival in Gentilly" share a "palimpsest" relation, the
novel is "about semiotics, about encoding and decoding signs."[21]

Samway offers a sound corrective to Hardy's frustration about "gaps,"

20. Hardy, *The Fiction of Walker Percy*, 35–49; Ralph C. Wood, "Percy as the Satirist
Satirized: *The Moviegoer*," a chapter in *The Comedy of Redemption: Christian Faith and Comic
Vision in Five American Novelists* (Notre Dame, 1988), 155–77.

21. Hardy, *The Fiction of Walker Percy*, 56; "Carnival in Gentilly" appeared in University
of Houston *Forum*, III (1960), 4–18; Patrick H. Samway, S.J., "Gaps and Codes: Walker
Percy's 'Carnival in Gentilly,' " *Shenandoah*, XLIII (Spring, 1993), 51, 54–55.

and there can be no doubt that *The Moviegoer* reflects Percy's interest in semiotics. Yet I find it equally valuable to look at Percy's first novel in light of his concern with the study of semiotics, "not texts and other coded sign utterances but the self which produces texts or hears sign utterances" (*LC*, 83). A first-person narrative, *The Moviegoer* is ostensibly "produced" by Binx Bolling. In the Epilogue, Binx makes the only reference to his production of the text when he says "Reticence, therefore, hardly having a place in a document of this kind, it seems as good a time as any to make an end" (*MG*, 237). It may prove useful, then, to take a semiotic look at the narrator himself.

I have already mentioned Binx's efforts to find a sign for himself by means of immanence and transcendence. I have also suggested that he ironizes his own attempts at such objectification. As a distancing tool, irony duplicates the space within the sign itself. Since irony creates a space between the ironist and the ironized, its expression by means of signs parallels the distance between the signifier and the signified at the very level of the sign. The "gaps" in the text, then, have a twofold origin. They arise as a result of the nature of the sign and as a consequence of Binx's ironic posture. When Binx speaks of his life as a perfect consumer, for example, the ironic tone with which he speaks distances him from the closure that such a life implies—*i.e.,* from the belief that the self can be informed by consumer items. Because his irony includes self-irony, he cannot close the gap between signifier and signified that such a sign for the self would offer. By means of irony, then, he paradoxically reinstates the unformulability of the self. What appears as a potential sign for the self is subverted by the narrative tone. Binx is left signless.

As ironist, Binx is especially adept at sizing up others. It is as though he cannot avoid seeing the despair of objectifying the self, the despair of everydayness.[22] Eddie Lovell, for instance, represents what Binx would be were he not an ironist, for Eddie exists solely in the realm of the immanent:

> Yes! Look at him. As he talks, he slaps a folded newspaper against his pants leg and his eye watches me and at the same time sweeps the terrain behind me, taking note of the slightest movement. A green truck turns down Bourbon

22. For an especially good treatment of Percy's use of this Heideggerian term, see Edward G. Lawry, "Literature as Philosophy," *The Monist,* LXIII (1980), 547–57.

Street; the eye sizes it up, flags it down, demands credentials, waves it on. A businessman turns in at the Maison Blanche Building; the eye knows him, even knows what he is up to. And all the while he talks very well. His lips move muscularly, molding words into pleasing shapes, marshalling arguments, and during the slight pauses are held poised, attractively everted in a Charles Boyer pout—while a little web of saliva gathers in a corner like the clear oil of a good machine. Now he jingles the coins deep in his pocket. No mystery here!—he is as cogent as a bird dog quartering a field. He understands everything out there and everything out there is something to be understood. (18–19)

According to Binx, Eddie exists as an organism in an environment. At once a "machine" and a "bird dog," he lives in the realm of signals. One thing announces another. In his posture of complete immanence, he has annulled the possibility of transcendence or distance. Eddie would have no difficulty describing himself, yet what he would not realize is that his description would more than likely be a signal. He would announce himself—as businessman, as husband, as planner—and thereby close any gap regarding his self-identity.

Yet it is Binx's posture that is interesting here. If Eddie observes and "sizes up" the terrain, Binx observes the observer. And if Eddie annuls the possibility of distance, Binx exists at a remove.[23] Eddie may be sunk in the immanent, but Binx is withdrawn from it. Neither displays the dialectic tension of the self. Rather, each has settled for a "deficient polarization"— one as consumer, the other as scientist. Without Binx's posture of detachment, of course, the book would not exist. There has to be distance. The question remains, though: How does one find the "right distance"?

The temptation to flee the unformulable self is great, and while Binx is aware of such evasions in Aunt Emily (a Catonist), Uncle Jules (a "canny creole"), Walter Wade (a social climber), Sam Yerger (a stoic novelist), and Mercer (an old retainer turned Rosicrucian), he nevertheless cultivates his own evasions. In admitting his own flight from self, he continually throws into question his designations of others. He cannot damn them in moral iniquity because his predicament is similar to, or worse than, theirs. In fact, as Binx encounters each character, he is drawn to their own resolution of

23. Richard Gray makes a comment similar to this in *Writing the South: Ideas of an American Region* (Cambridge, Eng., 1986), 257.

the predicament. While speaking with Eddie Lovell, he says "This is how one lives! My exile in Gentilly has been the worst kind of self-deception" (18). And when he visits with Aunt Emily he acknowledges that "this is where I belong after all" (26). He is drawn to the very despair he names. He seeks an answer to the autobiographical question, "Where am I?" Yet he senses the closure of objectification if he answers it in the fashion of Eddie or his aunt.

Binx avoids himself, to be sure, but his evasions are more self-consciously created. Borrowing terms from Kierkegaard's "Diapsalmata" in *Either/Or,* he practices what by now are familiar terms to students of Percy: rotations and repetitions. Binx defines rotation as "the experiencing of the new beyond the expectation of the experiencing of the new" (144). In rotation the unformulable self finds temporary relief from the dread of its unformulability by losing itself (closing itself) in the unexpected experience of the new. Rotation is an aesthetic category.[24]

Repetition, on the other hand, is both an aesthetic and an existential category. Binx's rather clumsy definition reads: "A repetition is the reenactment of past experience toward the end of isolating the time segment which has lapsed in order that it, the lapsed time, can be savored of itself and without the usual adulteration of events that clog time like peanuts in brittle" (79–80). Even though Binx succeeds where Constantin Constantius fails—Binx says he has "a successful repetition" (79)—he is nonetheless impoverished. Since Binx tries to "neutralize" time, to make it "like a yard of smooth peanut brittle" (80), his definition finds its place in the constancy of Kierkegaard's aesthetic sphere. In aesthetic repetition the unformulable self avoids the issue of its unformulability by viewing experience in closed, timeless "packages," as segments of lapsed time that can be savored of themselves, determinately formulated so as to provide the illusion that the self is also formulable. Such a repetition seeks to calm the "terrors of history" by neutralizing them. It is, in effect, the recollective posture outlined in Chapter 1.

But early drafts of *The Moviegoer* suggest that Percy had in mind existential repetition as well. A nearly illegible autograph note on the twenty-

----

24. Anthony Quagliano, "Existential Modes in *The Moviegoer*," Washington State University *Research Studies,* XLV (1977), 214–23.

sixth of fifty-seven pages of initial notes and outlines reads: "That [the?] repetition is more than just a savoring of something. It also makes the present possible."[25] Percy makes the distinction between aesthetic and existential repetition in "The Man on the Train" (*MB,* 83–100). He also mentions "Kierkegaard's distinction that true religious repetition has nothing to do with travel but is 'consciousness raised to the second power'" (*MB,* 96). My work is concerned with the latter two types, of course. Percy suggests that aesthetic repetition cannot make the present possible because it seeks the Great Moment of myth (*illud tempus*)—the romantic IT. It seeks another time. It is not insignificant that one short-story version of "Confessions of a Moviegoer" was subtitled "From the Diary of the Last Romantic." Binx is the last romantic because he has experienced the futility of seeking IT, some prepackaged experience of time. Binx recalls, for example, the melancholy he sank into after traveling with friends: "It seemed like a fine idea, sleeping in shelters or under the stars in the cool evergreens, and later hopping freights. In fact, this was what I was sure I wanted to do. But in no time at all I became depressed. The times we did have fun, like sitting around a fire or having a time with some girls, I had the feeling they were saying to me: 'How about this Binx? This is really it, isn't it, boy?', that they were practically looking up from their girls to say this" (41). In "Confessions of a Moviegoer" the moviegoer has more confidence in the IT. After coming out of a movie he reflects:

> This moment, the moment of the movies, the moment in which I live, is the Significant Moment. Where we [himself and actors] differ from other people is that they live in the moment as if it were like every other moment in their lives, a routine affair as if things and people were not any more worthy of noticing now than at any other time. The truth is that now everything is highly charged with meaning; everything is a Presence or a Power—that ordinary Brownstone there, that man on the subway: if the significance is not clear immediately, it soon will be. At any moment now, IT will begin.[26]

The romantic lives, not in the unformulable present, but in the expectation of the formulated IT. He sets before himself a prepackaged experience forever beyond his reach, yet one whose attainment, he believes, would cancel

---

25. Walker Percy, *The Moviegoer* typescript, A:1, p. 26, in Percy Papers, SHC.
26. Walker Percy, "Confessions of a Moviegoer," A:2, p. 11, in Percy Papers, SHC.

the dread of his unformulable self. Living in the expectation that such an experience will set him free, he awaits the day when fate will deliver it to him. In an interview with Jo Gulledge, Percy elaborates on what he means by the romantic: "Most people cannot conceive planning or initiating a course of action which would truly be an exercise of freedom. Although maybe they ought to. Most people are *thinking* of or are *waiting* for something magical to happen" (*Con*, 306). This comment underscores both the romantic's hope that salvation awaits him in the form of a prepackaged experience and Percy's contention that action in time (now!) provides an antidote to such romantic despair.

Binx, of course, is onto the futility of the romantic. In the final version of the novel, he eschews the romantic quest because, among other things, it "killed" his father.[27] And on the bus trip from Chicago to New Orleans, when he and Kate encounter a young man reading *The Charterhouse of Parma*, he directly states the romantic's dilemma: "The poor fellow. He has just begun to suffer from it, this miserable trick the romantic plays upon himself: of setting just beyond his reach the very thing he prizes" (215). The depression Binx experiences at times when he should feel the exhilaration of IT offers a clue to his search for new possibilities. Despite his self-consciously cultivated evasions, then, Binx holds out for something more, namely existential repetition. In his "writing" *The Moviegoer*, Binx evinces the movement of the autobiographer. Content neither with immanence nor transcendence, he looks for a place between that would make the present possible. One especially sly indication of this attitude occurs, once again, when Binx turns his irony upon himself.[28]

He recalls his freshman year of college when "it was extremely important to me to join a good fraternity." In an attempt to convince Binx that

27. For more on Percy and Romanticism, see Lewis A. Lawson, "English Romanticism . . . and 1930 Science in *The Moviegoer*," in *Following Percy: Essays on Walker Percy's Work* (Troy, N.Y., 1988), 83–107; Panthea Reid Broughton, "Walker Percy and the Myth of the Innocent Eye," in *Literary Romanticism in America*, ed. William L. Andrews (Baton Rouge, 1981), 94–108; Christina Murphy, " 'Exalted in This Romantic Place': Narrative Voice and the Structure of Walker Percy's *The Moviegoer*," *Publications of the Mississippi Philological Association* (1984), 55–68; and Richard Pindell, "Basking in the Eye of the Storm: The Esthetics of Loss in Walker Percy's *The Moviegoer*," *boundary 2*, IV (1975), 219–30.

28. All quotations cited here are taken from pages 36–38 in *MG*.

he should join the Deltas, the somewhat grandiose Walter Wade takes him aside and, although he says he will not "hand [Binx] the usual crap about this fraternity business," he does anyway: "When it comes to describing the fellows here, the caliber of the men, the bond between us, the meaning of this little symbol—he turned back his lapel to show the [fraternity] pin, . . ." then he dangles the IT in front of Binx: " 'I'll ask you a single question and then we'll go down. Did you or did you not feel a unique something when you walked into this house? I won't attempt to describe it. If you felt it, you already know exactly what I mean. If you didn't—!' Now Walter stands over me, holding his hat over his heart. 'Did you feel it, Binx?' " Caught up in the romanticism of Walter's rhetoric, Binx cannot resist joining the fraternity. Yet the rapture of his romantic capitulation ends in irony. From the context of his present consciousness, Binx reflects:

> As it turns out, I did not make them a good man at all. I managed to go to college four years without acquiring a single honor. When the annual came out, there was nothing under my picture but the letters $\Delta\Psi\Delta$—which was appropriate since I had spent the four years propped on the front porch of the fraternity house, bemused and dreaming, watching the sun shine through the Spanish moss, lost in the mystery of finding myself alive at such a time and place—and next to $\Delta\Psi\Delta$ my character summary: "Quiet but a sly sense of humor." (38)

In this passage Percy endows Binx with his own "quiet, sly sense of humor." For despite the banality of the situation and the ironic tone, what is at issue here is precisely "the meaning of this little symbol"—$\Delta\Psi\Delta$.

The deltas, of course, depict Percy's symbol for the irreducible triad of the sign. And psi provides the initial letter for "psyche," from which we derive our word for self or soul. Binx's own identity, then, is connected to the "meaning of this little symbol," the only entry underneath his picture. Although Binx did not make a good fraternity man, he nevertheless embodies the truth about the self for Percy: While the self (Ψ) cannot be encompassed by a sign (Δ), it nevertheless finds itself immured in sign use ($\Delta\Psi\Delta$) and so must look to the delta to understand itself. Binx manifests a repetitive posture as he watches "the sun shine through the Spanish moss, lost in the mystery of finding [himself] alive at such a time and place." It is important, first, that Binx "finds himself," and second that he finds himself "alive" and not "dead dead dead," as he so often finds others. The subtle self-irony provides the sign that opens the "mystery of time and place." Binx inhabits this time and place, and he finds the "right distance" to reveal himself— "lost"—in it. He finds himself, not in the Great Moment of myth, but in the ordinary everyday, which is quite different from the everydayness that precludes the possibility of a search. Thus, Binx is between (*inter esse*) the single sign (Δ) that can never formulate him and the sign use ($\Delta\Psi\Delta$) without which he can know nothing at all and that provides the best avenue, according to Percy, to know oneself. Like the autobiographer, Binx knows that the self can be captured only tentatively in sign use. His response to the autobiographical question, "Where am I?" places him ironically at no place—"lost in the mystery." In this "gap" of space and time he enters the present, the "now" that always has been but that now becomes possible. Furthermore, Binx's ironic naming and the distance it creates parallel the gap between the elements of the sign itself, a gap that has to be there "in order for the thing to be grasped" (*Con*, 227). While the romantic loses himself in the closure of his prepackaged experience, Binx finds himself in the openness of the sign.

Binx's subtle signification and irony in the narrative prevent the interpenetration of the signifier by the signified and leave him open to new possibilities. Although he slips out of the "right distance" from time to time in his ironic posture, he nevertheless manages what Paul A. Bové and Ronald Schleifer, following Kierkegaard, have called "mastered irony."[29] Unlike his father, who displays an "unmastered" irony and whose eyes "beyond a doubt . . . are ironical" (*MG*, 25) in the picture on Aunt Emily's mantelpiece, Binx manages the distance of his ironic posture. He stands between the fatal romantic irony of his father and the banal seriousness of Walter Wade. He maintains his repetitive posture, which is itself another term for "mastered irony."

But even so subtle an expression of existential repetition nevertheless

29. Bové, "Cleanth Brooks and Modern Irony," 727–59; Ronald Schleifer, "Irony and the Literary Past: *On the Concept of Irony* and *The Mill on the Floss*," in *Kierkegaard and Literature: Irony, Repetition, and Criticism*, ed. Ronald Schleifer and Robert Markley (Norman, Okla., 1984), 183–216. See also the editors' introduction, "Writing Without Authority and the Reading of Kierkegaard."

polarizes into the aesthetic in a work of art, as Percy says it must. It de-volves into something to savor, the merely interesting, as opposed to the interest that composes repetition (see *MB,* 97). What such subtlety de-mands, however, is a decision on the part of the reader. Although Percy says he "would like to think that [Binx] is an embodiment of a certain pa-thology of the twentieth century . . . it's an open question." The reader must decide whether Binx is "a nut" or whether he expresses an "authentic mood of the time" (*Con,* 302). Like Kierkegaard, Percy points to the exis-tential by means of the aesthetic. Such an attempt is bound to provide an ambiguous sign. Just as it is impossible to determine whether the "ambig-uous sienna color[ed] Negro" has received ashes on Ash Wednesday, the last day of the novel's action (before the Epilogue), so too it is impossible to close the gap in the sign that is the novel. In the openness of this sign, Percy allows for the possibility of repetition. Binx eschews a romantic and transcendent closure into form and seeks instead the possibilities of his own time. He will "listen to people, see how they stick themselves into the world, hand them along a ways in their dark journey and be handed along, and for good and selfish reasons" (*MG,* 233).

THE DISLOCATED SELF: LANGUAGE, PLACE, AND WILL BARRETT

To say that Percy's characters are dislocated offers nothing new to the body of scholarship surrounding his works. And to portray Will Barrett as an example of this dislocation is not to say that Percy's other characters do not suffer the same fate. Binx Bolling, Tom More, and Lancelot Lamar can all be seen as exiles in almost every aspect of their existence. Yet Will Barrett of *The Last Gentleman* is the only character whose story begins and ends outside of the South. Although Percy balked at the label "Southern Writer"—"would you describe John Cheever as being a Northern Writer?" (*MCon,* 223)—he nevertheless acknowledged that his novels, especially *The Moviegoer,* would not work without the backdrop of the South's rich tradi-tion: "Without the southern backdrop—Mississippi, Louisiana (New Or-leans)—the novel doesn't work—it doesn't work at *all.* Try to imagine Binx Bolling in Butte, Montana. There has to be a contrast between this very saturated culture in the south, on one hand, whether it's French, Creole, uptown New Orleans, or Protestant. It's a very dense society or culture which you need for Binx to collide with" (*Con*, 301). For Percy to remove a character from this fertile ground, then, suggests a degree of dislocation unequal to that of the other characters.

In one of his early interviews, Percy admits that Barrett is "a good deal sicker" than Binx, but, as with Binx, "the reader is free to see him as a sick man among healthy businessmen or as a sane pilgrim in a mad world" (*Con*, 13). Not only is Barrett "sicker," his story—both in *The Last Gentleman* and *The Second Coming*—is the only one written from the third-person point of view, an indication, perhaps, that Percy needs to distance himself from this addled young man in order to get the story straight. To further emphasize his dislocation, Percy withholds his name from the reader for the first ten pages of the novel. When he does give his name, he presents the reader with a multiple choice: "[his] name was Williston Bibb Barrett or Will Barrett or Billy Barrett."[30] And to complicate matters even more, the narrator most often refers to Barrett, not by his name, but as "the engineer."

John Edward Hardy has argued convincingly that the novel's opening, with its emphasis on place, is "clearly ironic." Not only is Will a "displaced" southerner living in New York, but the scene at Central Park, ostensibly constructed to provide a definite location for the action, nevertheless devolves into "no place . . . an anywhere and nowhere." This reading gains credibility when we learn some pages later that a spot in the southeast quadrant of the park has been marked as "ground zero," the center of a "series of concentric circles" (*LG*, 47), on a map depicting the explosion of a nerve-gas bomb. Barrett, then, is thrice removed from place, and he seeks a sign that will locate him in the world: "Often nowadays people do not know what to do and so live out their lives as if they were waiting for some sign or other. This young man was such a person" (6). With his telescope of "an unusual design" (3), this nameless, displaced southerner awaits a sign at ground zero of "no place."[31]

30. For more on this "exfoliation" of names, see Simone Vauthier, "Narrative Triangulation in *The Last Gentleman*," in *The Art of Walker Percy*, ed. Broughton, 69–95.

31. Hardy, *The Fiction of Walker Percy*, 59. For another analysis of this opening scene, see Lewis Lawson, "Will Barrett Under the Telescope," *Southern Literary Journal*, XX (1988), 16–41;   See Martin Luschei, the chapter "Ground Zero to Santa Fe," in *The Sovereign Wayfarer*, 111–68.

The telescope is outfitted with a camera so that Barrett might photograph a peregrine falcon he had seen the day before. It does not return, so Barrett begins to dismantle the telescope. Yet "being of both a scientific and a superstitious turn of mind and therefore always on the lookout for chance happenings which lead to great discoveries, he had to have a last look" (5). What he finds proves to be the chance event he has been waiting for, the sign "as a consequence [of which] the rest of his life was to be changed" (3).

The event that changes Barrett's life is also, of course, the incident that sets the novel in motion. The passage merits close inspection: "There in the telescope sat a woman, on a park bench, a white woman dark as a gypsy. She held a tabloid. Over her shoulder he read: '. . . parley fails' " (5). The woman turns out to be Rita Vaught, and we learn that she leaves messages at the park bench for Kitty Vaught, the second woman Barrett sees through his telescope and with whom he falls in love.

Since it is the instrument through which Barrett sees his life-changing sign, the telescope itself merits analysis. We know very little about it at this point in the novel, only that it was of "unusual design" and that it could be fitted with a camera. This latter feature is noteworthy because it doubles the telescope's capacity for observation. The telescope narrows and amplifies the field of vision while the camera stabilizes and freezes it into a single image. We learn later that when Barrett purchased the telescope, he had looked upon it as something that would, like the sign it reveals, change him: "his life depended on it." The telescope also suits Barrett's scientific/ magical temperament: "[its] lenses did not transmit light merely. They penetrated into the heart of things" (29). The instrument both reflects and creates the world in the "brilliant theater of its lenses" (5). In so doing, it recovers things. When Barrett turns his instrument toward a building, for example, "it was better than having the bricks there before him. They gained in value. Every grain and crack and excrescence became available. Beyond a doubt, he said to himself, this proves that bricks, as well as other things, are not as accessible as they used to be. Special measures were needed to recover them. The telescope recovered them" (31). The telescope is Barrett's instrument for recovering and discovering the world. Through its lenses, Barrett knows the world.

The character and power of this "unusual" instrument—it is the agent in many of the passages that describe it—suggest that it can be read as an analogue or a metaphor for the novel. Like the subtle expression of Percy's linguistic philosophy in Binx's ΔΨΔ, the description of the telescope suggests Percy's views about the diagnostic function of the novel. The telescope, after all, is a scientific instrument, and as I tried to show in Chapter 1, Percy uses the novel "scientifically."

Like the telescope, the novel magnifies a section of the world; it wrests it from its usual context so that it might be seen afresh and named. The novel strives to recover the world. Later in the story, when Barrett is on the road with Jamie, Kitty's sixteen-year-old brother who is dying, he observes a man on a "fifty-foot Chris-Craft beat up the windy Intercoastal." He calls Jamie over to see what he sees in the telescope:

> "Look how he pops his jaw and crosses his legs with the crease of his britches pulled out of the way."
> "Yes," said Jamie, registering and savoring what the engineer registered and savored. *Yes, you and I know something the man in the Chris-Craft will never know.* (162, Percy's emphasis)

Jamie and Will meet in what they see through the telescope in the same fashion as reader and writer meet in the reading of a novel. We know more about Will Barrett than Will knows about himself. The novel establishes an intersubjective community between reader and writer in its very naming. And since a name is also a sign, the novel also resists closure or stasis.

It is significant, then, that Barrett's ostensible use for the telescope, to photograph the peregrine falcon, fails. Made versatile by the addition of the camera, the telescope promises not only to magnify the falcon but also to stabilize it, to close it within the rigid boundaries of a photograph. That Barrett does not capture the falcon on film both foreshadows his coming peregrinations and points to the limits of the novel itself. Like the falcon, Barrett is himself a sign of instability. Just as the falcon has "abandoned its natural home in the northern wilderness and taken up residence on top of the hotel," so Barrett has left the South and taken up residence in the New York City YMCA. Neither remains, however. The "peregrine did not return to his perch" (5), and Barrett soon begins his travels, which end in the "no place" of the desert. Just as the telescope sees—but cannot place—the falcon, so the novel names—but does not place—Barrett. Both are wanderers, pilgrims without a home, displaced. The names they are given place them "nowhere."[32]

But if the ostensible purpose for Barrett's using his telescope fails, the manifest purpose does not. The telescope, again like the novel, serves its voyeuristic function well. It observes without being observed. It amplifies unobtrusively.[33] At one point Barrett declares his appreciation of English detective stories, "especially the sort which . . . depict the hero as perfectly disguised or perfectly hidden. . . . Englishmen like to see without being seen" (161–62). The telescope is the novelist's tool par excellence. If neither the novel nor the telescope can place their respective pilgrims from their concealed viewpoints, then both can at least help to name this same predicament. What the telescope does observe, and what the novel ultimately points to as well, is precisely what Barrett sees when he takes his one last look: ". . . parley fails."

This rich, polyvalent fragment would deserve little consideration were it not in a novel by Percy, and at the all-important beginning.[34] Parley derives from the French *parler* and the ecclesiastical Latin *parabolare,* both meaning "to speak." *Parabolare,* in turn, derives from the Latin *parabola,* a speech, from which we get the word parable. In English, parley can be used either as a verb, "to have a conference or discussion," or as a noun, "a talk or conference for the purpose of discussing a specific matter."[35] Percy is especially sly in his use of the term, for the fragment remains so open that it encompasses both the etymological and the usage definitions.

Since the word appears as a part of a tabloid headline, it apparently refers to a meeting or conference. The time of the novel is never precisely set. There is a mention of John Kennedy's death, and one scene refers indirectly to the riots that occurred at the University of Mississippi after desegregation. So the time would appear to be the early 1960s. The fragment,

32. As in T. S. Eliot's *Four Quartets,* the play on "nowhere"/"now-here" is intended. To be "now-here" is precisely the autobiographical and repetitive stance. See Chapter 1.

33. On the subtle beauty of Percy's prose, see especially James Dickey's review of *The Last Gentleman* in *American Scholar,* XXXVII (1968), 524.

34. Percy toiled over all his works, but especially over the beginnings, as the manuscripts at the SHC display.

35. Etymology and definitions taken from *Webster's New World Dictionary* (1984), New York.

then, could refer to any number of failed parleys that undoubtedly took place during that era: about the mounting Cold War, about the riots themselves, about the escalation of the United States' involvement in the Vietnam conflict, anything.

Given Percy's interest in the language phenomenon, however, a more fruitful reading arises from evidence inside the novel itself and from his comments in the "Primer" about the devolution of the sign and placement. What we learn as *The Last Gentleman* progresses is that Will Barrett finds himself in the midst of a number of failed parleys, in every sense of the word. Will's thwarted relationship with Kitty, their aborted attempts at lovemaking (a connotative meaning of parley), Will's relation to Dr. Gamow (his psychoanalyst), the relationship between Kitty and Rita Vaught (Kitty's overseer and general "helper" who displays ambiguous sexual intentions), between Rita and Sutter Vaught (Rita's ex-husband, a failed doctor turned pornographer), between Will and Sutter, between Sutter and Val Vaught (a nun who works with the rural Tyree people), between Will and his father, and even the picaresque adventures of Will with Forney Aiken and company, with the ladies on the highway, and with the black bar-owner and the white policemen in his hometown—all suggest the centrality of this tabloid fragment. These relationships display the failure of speaking. Words are bankrupt. The one notable exception to this general collapse is the relationship between Jamie and Will, whose co-celebration of what is develops in light of their complementarity: "Jamie read books of great abstractness. . . . The engineer, on the other hand, read books of great particularity" (*LG*, 162).

Meanwhile, this breakdown of words has to do with the devolution of the sign. When the signified becomes entombed by the signifier and when the repetitive posture of primordial sign use is lost, intersubjectivity in consciousness also wanes. In other words, when speaking fails, love fails. The problem is not that the characters do not try to speak. On the contrary, words flow freely between them. It is the peculiar posture from which they speak that concerns Percy. Since he explores the conditions that accompany the end of the modern world and the dawn of the postmodern one, he also examines the causes and effects of the breakdown of language. In the words of the epigram:

We know now that the modern world is coming to an end . . . at the same time, the unbeliever will emerge from the fogs of secularism. He will cease to reap benefit from the values and forces developed by the very Revelation he denies . . . Loneliness in faith will be terrible. Love will disappear from the face of the public world, but the more precious will be that love which flows from one lonely person to another . . . the world to come will be filled with animosity and danger, but it will be a world open and clean.[36]

The posture that creates the condition for the failure of words, love, and faith evolves from an imbalance of immanence and transcendence. For Percy the postmodern world bears witness to transcendence or immanence taken separately, or it evinces some strange hybrid of the two, but it has lost any sense of organic unity between them. With such a radical disjunction, Percy suggests, it is inevitable that parleys often fail.

Rita, for example, illustrates one facet of this extensive bankruptcy. Since she blends immanence and transcendence from a transcendent posture, she embodies a Hegelian, scientific-humanist attitude. Her "mode of reentry" consists of a general beneficence that masks an essential isolation. Kitty is onto her—"I knew exactly how to make her like me!" (114)—although she remains awed by her:

> Rita is a remarkable person. . . . She showed me something I never dreamed existed. Two things. First, the way she devoted herself to the Indians. I never saw anything like it. They adored her. I saw one child's father try to kneel and kiss her foot. Then she showed me how a thing can be beautiful. She kept Shakespeare's sonnets by her bed. And she actually read them. Listen to this, she would say, and she would read it. And I could hear it the way she heard it! Bare ruin'd choirs, where late the sweet birds sang. Poetry: who'd have thought it? We went for walks. I listened to her but then (is this bad?) I began to see how much she was enjoying teaching me. (114–15)

Percy seems to have endowed Rita with a part of his adoptive father's character. Although she does not exhibit the stoical melancholia of William Alexander Percy—this facet of his character is given to Will's father, as I will discuss below—it is significant that Kitty's description of her parallels Percy's own comments about "Uncle Will." In the introduction to *Lanterns*

36. The epigram is from Romano Guardini, *The End of the Modern World: A Search for Orientation,* trans. Joseph Theman and Herbert Burke (New York, 1956), 68, 124, 132, 128.

on the Levee, Percy tells of the way Will Percy used to read to him or play music for him. He began, he says, to see things the way his teacher saw them: "The teacher points and says *Look;* the response is *Yes, I see.*" He also calls Will Percy "the most extraordinary man I have ever known."[37]

Like Will Percy's beneficence toward the blacks in the Delta, Rita's work with the Indians is indeed generous. It evolves from the stoic's attitude of noblesse oblige, something which Walker addresses in "Stoicism in the South." The stoic's attitude, Percy argues, essentially isolates him. His "generosity" masks the sentiment that doing others "an injustice would be to defile the inner fortress which [is] oneself." One cares for others not because they are individuals but because not caring for them would wound "the wintry kingdom of self" (*Signposts,* 85). The stoic's end is a solipsism that seeks to protect the self from the vicissitudes of history. Rita's name for the camper in which Jamie and Will travel—"Ulysses"—and her comment on that name point to her transcendent posture: "He was meant to travel beyond the borders of the Western world and bring us home" (*LG,* 96).

Will's home, like that of his classical predecessor, is Ithaca, and one wonders if Percy seeks the same stability that Jeffrey M. Perl argues the modernists found in their return to the classics. Lewis Lawson has shown how women in *The Moviegoer* find parallels in classical literature, yet his argument would not seem to support the sort of return of which Perl writes. Writing about *The Moviegoer* and Plato's Allegory of the Cave, Lawson contends that for Plato "only the dutiful return [from their view of the ideal] to live among the wall-watchers, and they only to instruct. It is otherwise with the Percy movement. . . . Unlike Plato's movement, Percy's does not culminate with a communion that can be attained by the mastery of an abstract scheme. An individual remains a moviegoer, or a wall-watcher, as long as he distances himself from his ultimate world by the very way in which he looks at it." For his part, William V. Spanos holds that Perl, like Hegel and Toynbee, "domesticates" the idea of return, and so it finds its source in an atemporal dialectic rather than in time. As for the

---

37. Walker Percy, Introduction to *Lanterns on the Levee,* by William Alexander Percy (Baton Rouge, 1973), xi, xviii.

dutiful Will Percy, so for Rita: intersubjectivity fails, and the world slips away in the code of noblesse oblige.[38]

Sutter exemplifies a different permutation of the insolvency of words. As a physician he participates in the transcendent scientific community. He has even published a paper, an act that confirms his initiation into that sovereign society.[39] The title of the essay points to his own predicament with placement on the immanent-transcendent continuum: *The Incidence of Post-orgasmic Suicide in Male University Graduate Students.* The paper itself is divided into two sections with subtitles: "Genital Sexuality as the Sole Surviving Communication Channel Between Transcending-Immanent Subjects," and "The Failure of Coitus as a Mode of Reentry into the Sphere of Immanence from the Sphere of Transcendence" (See *LG,* 65).

Sutter has recognized the radical bifurcation that has occurred in the wake of the failure of words, and he exists as its most poignant exemplar. Percy argues in *Lost in the Cosmos* that a corollary of such a collapse is the ascendance of sex in various forms. When signs devolve, when the transcendence that sign use provides falters, the only avenues to transcendence become sex and violence. It is notable that almost every failed parley cited above involves a correlate to sex. The exceptions—the scene at the hometown bar and Will's relationship with his father, which ends in his father's suicide—find their correlate in violence. Yet an element of sex, too, exists in the story of Mr. Barrett's suicide. On the night of his death, he denounces the fact that his "class" had become "the fornicators and bribers" (330) they once opposed, and he leaves Will confused on the business of lady and whore (180). In *The Second Coming,* Percy unites sex and violence more trenchantly in Barrett's reflections on his father's suicide, indicating

38. Jeffrey M. Perl, *The Tradition of the Return* (Princeton, 1984); Lewis Lawson, "Walker Percy's Novels: Paradise Lost, Paradise Regained," paper presented at the symposium "The Achievement of Walker Percy," April 20, 1991, Jackson, Miss., sponsored by the University Press of Mississippi; Lewis Lawson, "Walker Percy's *The Moviegoer:* Cinema as Cave," in *Following Percy,* 91–92; Spanos, *Repetitions,* 261, note; see also Lewis Lawson, "Walker Percy's Southern Stoic," and "*The Moviegoer* and the Stoic Heritage" in *Following Percy.* See also Allen, *Walker Percy.*

39. The figures of speech are not inappropriate since Percy writes in the "Primer" that "the scientist is the prince and sovereign of the age" (*LC,* 116).

perhaps a confirmation of his Percy's theories and a breakthrough to under-standing his own father's death.[40]

Sutter becomes a pornographer because he is trapped in the transcen-dence of his science. He seeks reentry to the immanent realm by means of what he sees as the purely immanent, sex. Thus, he manifests a strange hy-brid of the immanent-transcendent dialectic, an angelism-bestialism that Percy will develop more fully in *Love in the Ruins*. Yet Sutter despairs in his Jekyll-and-Hyde existence. When this mode of reentry fails him, he consid-ers violence. He contemplates suicide.

It is useful to point out again that Percy *explores* the postmodern pre-dicament with regard to place. *The Last Gentleman* evolves not so much as a jeremiad, although its tone in parts can be seen as cantankerous, but as a search for possibilities. For Percy a pilgrim finds his end only *at the end* of his life. That some characters reach a dead end suggests either that they have quit their search for new prospects or that the logical conclusion of the postures they embrace bears witness to death-in-life. Alienation and home-lessness are natural states, not psychological disorders. Although an adept satirist, Percy does not condemn characters who try to find a home, not even Lancelot Lamar. Rather, as Louis Rubin has argued, he writes of them from the standpoint of having been there himself: "Walker's [fiction] is not Jansenist; it is not written from a position of theological privilege located far above the struggle, judging the poor deluded sinners and consigning them to the fire. . . . [He] includes himself among the sinful."[41] The posture that remains most open to possibility is that of the pilgrim, one who is at home in homelessness, such as the addled wayfarer of *The Last Gentleman*.

Will Barrett not only drifts into one failed parley after another, but finds himself, quite literally, in the middle of them. Perhaps the first indi-cation of this middle state manifests itself with Dr. Gamow's "ambiguous chair": "[Dr. Gamow] learned a great deal about a patient from the way he sat in the chair. Some would walk in and sit straight up, swivel around to face the doctor across the desk like a client consulting a lawyer. Others

40. Barrett's description of his father's suicide can be found in *SC,* 148–49. For a good treatment of suicide in *SC,* see J. Gerald Kennedy, "The Semiotics of Memory: Suicide in *The Second Coming," Delta* (Montpellier, France), XIII (1981), 103–25.

41. Louis D. Rubin, Jr., "Walker Percy: 1916–1990," *Southern Literary Journal,* XXIII (1990), 6.

would stretch out and swivel away to face the corner in conventional analytic style. It was characteristic of the engineer that he sat in the ambiguous chair ambiguously: leaving it just as it was, neither up nor down, neither quite facing Dr. Gamow nor facing away" (*LG,* 31–32). Neither new-style client (à la Carl Rogers) nor old-style analysand, Barrett resists formulation. That he abruptly terminates his analysis suggests the limits of the psychoanalytic process, about which Percy has written cogently elsewhere (*Signposts,* 251–62). Although he tells himself that he will "engineer the future of [his] life according to the scientific principles and the self-knowledge [he has] so arduously gained from five years of analysis" (*LG,* 41), the narrator's very tone betrays him. The "scientific principles" of analysis cannot account for this pilgrim's alienation.

But the "ambiguous chair" is only one of many examples of Will's "being between." After he declares his love for Kitty and wins the affection of Jamie, he steps between almost all of the established relationships in the Vaught family. Rita considers him a rival for the attentions of Kitty and so devises a plan that allows him to travel with Jamie. Unknown to Will, Rita's interests focus on separating the new lovers. But Pappy (Mr. Vaught) has already proposed a plan to Will, and so Will finds himself between both Kitty and Rita and between the wishes of Pappy and Rita. Sutter, who wants to take Jamie to die in the desert of Santa Fe and who is something of a father figure for Will, has no use either for serving as Will's guide or for his sister's (Val's) desire to see Jamie baptized. Val, however, has charged Barrett with that very task. Will, then, is placed between Sutter's nihilism and Val's faith.

Will is also caught between the present and his past. Because he is subject to amnesia, fugues, and déjà vu, he is disoriented in time. He often forgets, but when he does remember he recalls "the remote past first" (57), often unwittingly. Time and again he experiences unannounced intrusions of the past into his present consciousness. Such intrusions mimic, in a sense, the autobiographical act. Will seeks to piece his life together. At this point in the novel, however, since the recollections are unwilled, Barrett seems unaware of this latent autobiographical impulse. Still, we know more about Barrett than he does about himself, so the autobiographical perspective remains open to us. In a way Will serves as his own analyst. He doesn't necessarily "engineer" his life, but he endeavors to be what Dr. Gamow tried to be to him: "it was easy to believe that . . . he served his patients best as artificer and shaper, receiving the raw stuff of their misery and handing it back in a public and acceptable form" (35). The reference to Wallace Stevens' idea of shaping and making complements an earlier reference to Freud: "A German physician once remarked that in the lives of people who suffer emotional illness he had noticed the presence of *Lücken* or gaps. As he studied the history of a particular patient he found whole sections missing, like a book with blank pages." Although Freud was Austrian, the allusion seems fairly clear.[42] The psychiatrist fills in the gaps, gives shape to the "raw material" that is a person's life, as Freud did in his case histories. The psychiatrist, in other words, fashions the story (the *parabola*) of the patient. He writes the patient's life.

The danger of such a role—a reason this parley might fail—resides in the fact that a patient may lose sovereignty over that same story. While analysis ostensibly proposes a recovery of patients' lost sovereignty, the process may result in their further alienation. When the psychiatrist insists too strongly on filling in blank pages, on fashioning a well-made story, the story may serve the wishes of the analyst rather than the needs of the patient. In the case of Dora, for example, Freud seems less concerned with Dora as an individual than with Dora as an instance of his own theories. He masters her story.[43]

Commenters on Percy's fiction often note the pleasure he takes in turning Freud upside down. Percy himself once admitted that this was one of his narrative strategies (see *Con,* 68). That Percy writes the story of a character with severe gaps in his memory suggests his attempt to endow Barrett with his own sovereignty. As his experience with the "ambiguous chair" implies, Barrett is not made to fit any theory that places the ideal before the actual. For Percy such theories are bankrupt: they lead only to romanticism and despair. Percy struggles against the bankruptcy of words by telling a story whose words point to their own inadequacy—Barrett himself is a romantic—yet that nevertheless provide the only means by which to know

42. *LG,* 12; Lawson, "Will Barrett Under the Telescope," 17.

43. Sigmund Freud, *Dora: An Analysis of a Case of Hysteria* (New York, 1963). For a parallel to slave narratives see James Olney, " 'I Was Born': Slave Narratives, Their Status as Autobiography and as Literature," in *The Slave's Narrative,* ed. Charles Davis and Henry Louis Gates (Oxford, Eng., 1985), 148–75.

anything at all. That Will Barrett quits analysis even though he still suffers from gaps points to his inchoate sense of the perils of the analytic process.

At the same time, however, Will recognizes the necessity of fashioning a story, and he looks to those his "radar" tells him know better than he. Sutter is such a person. Frustrated that Sutter won't play analyst for him, Will reflects: "Damnation, if I am such an old story to him, why doesn't he tell me how the story comes out?" (223). Sutter, however, recognizes that any attempt to satisfy this ubiquitous, although impossible, desire would serve only to alienate Barrett further. In his casebook he fills in some of the pages for Will. Sutter carries on a dialogue with Val, whom he imagines speaking to Barrett:

> Look, Barrett, your trouble is due not to a disorder of your organism but to the human condition, that you do well to be afraid and you do well to forget everything which does not pertain to your salvation. That is to say, your amnesia is not a symptom. So you say: Here is the piece of news you have been waiting for, and you tell him. What does Barrett do? He attends in that eager flattering way of his and at the end of it he might even say *yes!* But he will receive the news from his high seat of transcendence as one more item of psychology, throw it into his immanent meat-grinder, and wait to see if he feels better.[44]

Sutter leaves Will to his *Lücken,* and Barrett is left to piece together the story of himself as he shuttles between the past and present.

One of the main gaps in Barrett's story, of course, concerns his father's death. Fragments of the incident recur throughout the course of the narrative. But once Sutter takes Jamie to Santa Fe, leaving Barrett to travel through the South on his own, he is all the more haunted by déjà vu and intrusions of his past. When he arrives at his hometown, Ithaca, Mississippi, and when he finds himself before his childhood home, the place of his father's death, the story demands form more insistently. Barrett becomes an autobiographer—one who seeks a story (and thus a place) for his self and his life. Although his father has won a victory over the "bribers and fornicators," all is not well. The boy and his father stroll outside in the night as they listen to Brahms:

---

44. *LG,* 353–54. Sutter's comments about news parallel the title essay of *The Message in the Bottle,* in which Percy develops his distinction between knowledge and news. See *MB,* 119–49.

> As he turned to leave, the youth called out to him. "Wait."
>
> "What?"
>
> "Don't leave."
>
> "I'm just going to the corner."
>
> But there was a dread about this night, the night of victory. (Victory is the saddest thing of all, said the father.) The mellowness of Brahms had gone over-ripe, the victorious serenity of the Great Horn Theme was false, oh fake fake. Underneath all was unwell. (*LG,* 331)

The elder Barrett ultimately states his philosophy of life: "In the last analysis you are alone" (331). Although Will repeats his plea several times—*Wait. Don't leave!*—his father nevertheless kills himself. But the story has finally taken shape in Will's memory.

Some years later, as he stands at the place of this horrible memory, past and present merge such that the future seems possible to him. His hand strays to an old iron-horse hitching post around which an oak tree has grown. As he reflects, Will briefly adopts a repetitive posture:

> *Wait.* While his fingers explored the juncture of iron and bark, his eyes narrowed as if he caught a glimmer of light on the cold iron skull. *Wait.* I think he was wrong and that he was looking in the wrong place. No, not he but the times. The times were wrong and one looked in the wrong place. It wasn't his fault because that was the way he was and the way the times were, and there was no other place a man could look. It was the worst of times, a time of fake beauty and fake victory. *Wait.* He had missed it! It was not in the Brahms that one looked and not in solitariness and not in the old sad poetry but—he wrung out his ear—but here, under your nose, here in the very curiousness and drollness and extraness of the iron and the bark that—he shook his head— that— (332)

Louis D. Rubin, Jr., has written beautifully on the significance of this superb passage. What Will realizes as his hand explores the "juncture of iron and bark" is that "his father's ideal of aristocratic virtue, however nobly motivated, was actually a romantic escape from the compromised actuality of human life in time." That Brahms is playing in the background only reinforces the elder Barrett's isolation. For the music sets up a romantic ideal of perfection that in its "massive harmonics pronounce[s] an ultimate resolution superior to merely human difficulties and leaving no further occasion for striving or disruption." The music, Rubin argues, sets up an ideal of perfection that parallels the supposed ethical perfection of the southern aristocrat. The victory over the "rabble" and the music's own victory are fake because each points to a static perfection (*in illo tempore*) that annuls a "vital relationship with ongoing experience"— change in time.[45]

The era of the southern aristocrat, if there ever was one, has waned; and although Rubin does not make the connection, to try to hold on to such standards reinforces what Kierkegaard calls the despair to will to be oneself in despair. In a passage that closely parallels the plight of Mr. Barrett, Kierkegaard writes: "In despair the self wants to enjoy the total satisfaction of making itself into itself, of developing itself, of being itself; it wants to have the honor of this poetic, masterly construction, the way it has understood itself. And yet, in the final analysis, what it understands by itself is a riddle; in the very moment when it seems that the self is closest to having the building completed, it can arbitrarily dissolve the whole thing into nothing."[46] Mr. Barrett, of course, dissolves the edifice at the moment of both his and the music's victory. Like so many in the South who place the ideal before the actual, Mr. Barrett cannot sustain the tension of the now—the "being between" of the new age, the *inter esse* of the autobiographer.

His son, however, is still building his edifice, not a "poetic, masterly construction," not a "well-made story" that has no gaps. Rather, from his being between past and present, between the failed parleys of the Vaught family and, finally, between Father Boomer and Jamie at the story's conclusion, Barrett holds out, however unwittingly, for the possibility that "nowhere" might provide. That Barrett ultimately "misses," as Percy says, the significance both of Jamie's baptism and of his experience in front of his father's house does not devalue the signs themselves. For in the telescope that is the novel, the reader sees and knows something that Barrett does not. We see him as a fledgling autobiographer, capable of living *now*, without the whole story. This parley succeeds in its failure.

45. Louis D. Rubin, Jr., "The Boll Weevil, the Iron Horse, and the End of the Line," in *A Gallery of Southerners,* by Louis D. Rubin (Baton Rouge, 1982), 210, 211, 213. See also Linda Whitney Hobson, " 'Watching, Listening and Waiting': The Mode of the Seeker in Walker Percy's Fiction," *Southern Literary Journal,* XX (1988), 43–50.

46. Kierkegaard, *The Sickness unto Death,* 67ff., 69–70.

3

Repetition and *Bios:* Surviving Life in a Century of Gnosticism and Death

In the Flora Levy Lecture he delivered in the spring of 1991, Lewis Simpson recalled his burgeoning relationship with Walker Percy.[1] Built largely on an exchange of letters in which Simpson solicited contributions for *The Southern Review,* their association was, as Simpson characterized it, "professional." Yet they sometimes exchanged personal notes as well. Percy once responded to Simpson's "note of congratulations on his seventieth birthday" with the following: "I've got news for you. It's not all bad being in your 71st year. So you young fellows can relax. As a matter of fact, I feel it's a gift, a free ride. Nobody in my family ever lived so long. What it [takes] is Early Times and clean living." Simpson entered his seventy-first year less

---

1. The as-yet unpublished lecture, "Walker Percy's Vision of the Modern World," was delivered at the University of Southwestern Louisiana on March 7, 1991.

than two months later. He notes, however, that there was more of a "generational concord between Walker and me than the coincidental proximity of our birthdays." He and Percy shared the "drama of a generational sensibility." Based on an early exposure "to the density of the modern European literary mind" as it developed after the catastrophe of the First World War and the period between the world wars, they both participated in a "generational cultural dialectic," which held forth the possibility of either apocalyptic "doom" or a "recovery of memory and history."

Having experienced this dialectic in their reading, both men express it also in their writing. In *The Dispossessed Garden,* for example, Simpson cogently explores the possibility for the recovery of memory and history in the face of modernity. And in his works, Percy strives to retain the unity of the dialectic. For him apocalypse implies recovery. Destruction opens the possibility for renewal: "The prospect [of the ultimate catastrophe] gets one's attention. . . . If the Bomb is going to fall any minute, all things become possible, even love."[2]

Percy's comments reiterate what he writes in "The Loss of the Creature." In this essay he contends that science and romanticism have so entombed the "creature" in theory—a prepackaged IT—that it takes the destruction of everyday contexts to recover the actual. Thus, the "savage" in Huxley's *Brave New World* stands in an ideal posture for recovery: "[When he] stumbles across a volume of Shakespeare in some vine-grown ruins and squats on a potsherd to read it, [he] is in a fairer way of getting at a sonnet than the Harvard sophomore taking English Poetry II" (*MB*, 56). The ruins allow a recovery of what everyday contexts too often foreclose.[3] Herein rests the de-structive project of Percy—not a nihilistic doom, of course, but a shattering of everydayness so that the everyday, which has been, now becomes.

When Percy tells Simpson that he feels his seventy-first year is a "free

2. Lewis P. Simpson, *The Dispossessed Garden* (Athens, 1975); Patrick H. Samway, S.J., "An Interview with Walker Percy," *America,* February 15, 1986, p. 122; see also Ciuba, *Books of Revelations* and Lois Parkinson Zamora, *Writing the Apocalypse: Historical Vision in Contemporary U.S. and Latin American Fiction,* especially the chapter "Apocalypse and Renewal: Walker Percy and the U.S. South" (Cambridge, Mass., 1989), 120–47.

3. Jonathan Culler takes issue with Percy on this point. See his review "Man the Symbol-Monger," *Yale Review,* LXV (1976), 264.

ride," that "nobody in my family ever lived so long," he seems to evince a blend of doom and recovery, or at least of ruefulness and celebration. On the one hand, he exults in the very possibility of joking about his age. Yet his exultation is darkened by a shadow of regret. He seems to brood over the very necessity of surviving in this era, something that many of his progenitors, most notably his father, could not do. As Jay Tolson's biography and Wyatt-Brown's history make clear, Percy had good reason for both sentiments. A scion of the Percy line, he inherited a proclivity toward melancholia, depression, and suicide. As a son of the South, he struggled against a romantic tradition that placed the ideal before the real. Tolson shows how Percy watched his father try—and ultimately fail—to live up to the southern code of honor, loyalty, and nobility. He likewise reveals the despair that characterized his adoptive father's assessment of the twentieth century, an evaluation that denied the possibility of change in time.[4] Percy celebrates his seventy-first year because he has overcome both the southern code and his family. He holds to a view of himself as a "pilgrim in the ruins," a seeker of the possibility of recovery amidst the "catastrophe" and "doom" of the twentieth century. He is a survivor of what he often called this "century of death."[5]

I have already tried to show how Percy's characterization of the age holds true with regard to its exaltation of science. As a result of the misapprehension of the scientific method, "[creatures] are rendered invisible by a shift of reality from concrete thing to theory which Whitehead has called the fallacy of misplaced concreteness. It is the mistaking of an idea, a principle, an abstraction, for the real. As a consequence, the 'specimen' is seen as less real than the theory of the specimen" (*MB*, 58). This "loss of the creature" characterizes the "malaise" of the age. In *The Moviegoer*, Binx Bolling defines malaise in these same terms. It is "the pain of loss. The world is lost to you, the world and the people in it, and there remains only you and the world and you no more able to be in the world than Banquo's ghost" (*MG*, 120). Part of this loss, another facet of the dis-ease of the twentieth

4. See William Alexander Percy, *Lanterns on the Levee;* see also Gray, *Writing the South,* 251–70.

5. In his interviews and essays Percy called the twentieth century many things, most of them subsumable under the title I have cited.

century, can be related to the resurgence of Gnostic thought, a stepbrother to the deification of science, and a stance against which Percy's works, as autobiography, struggle. For if autobiography displays the repetitive movement that brings one into a relation of interest in time, then it moves away from an atemporal and otherworldly Gnostic purity and into the vicissitudes of history. The autobiographer, like Percy's protagonists, finds his place in the *inter esse* of repetition.

With characteristic lucidity, Cleanth Brooks and Lewis Lawson have already pointed out how Gnosticism finds a place in Percy's fiction, especially in *Lancelot*.[6] I do not need to retrace their arguments. Instead, I hope to show that Percy's corpus, fiction and essays, counters a Gnostic attitude, especially as it manifests itself in the angelism/bestialism of the Weimar Republic and the Nazi Holocaust. Before I can do this, however, the term demands some stability. For Gnosticism, like repetition and autobiography, defies facile definition. Christopher Lasch, for example, has written that Gnosticism "remains an elusive thing," a "hydra-headed" movement. The scholarly attempt to delimit it, he argues, leads only to a "proliferation of definitions" that grow out of a more fundamental "controversy about its origins." In a thorough and illuminating article, Henri-Charles Puech likewise points to the difficulty of arriving at a stable view of Gnosticism, and he acknowledges that part of its elusiveness results from a confusion about its roots.

Puech shows that although it was long considered solely a Christian heresy, Gnosticism "came to be understood as a determinate genus, widely distributed in both space and time, of which heretical Christian Gnosis represented only a particular species."[7] For Puech, "determinate genus" refers not to a single expression of Gnostic thought; rather, it provides a "category of philosophico-religious thought" for understanding the multiplicity of expressions or "styles" that can be subsumed under the name *Gnostic*. Although broad and diverse in its manifestations, Gnosticism nevertheless

6. Cleanth Brooks, "Walker Percy and Modern Gnosticism," in *The Art of Walker Percy,* ed. Broughton 260–72; Lewis Lawson, "The Gnostic Vision in *Lancelot*" and "Gnosis and Time in *Lancelot*" both in *Following Percy,* 196–209, 210–26.

7. Christopher Lasch, "Probing Gnosticism and its Modern Derivatives," *New Oxford Review,* LVII (December, 1990), 6, 7; Henri-Charles Puech, "Gnosis and Time," in *Man and Time,* ed. Joseph Campbell (New York, 1957), 54.

exhibits a common "attitude," itself difficult to define: "If it were possible to [define it] in a few words, we should say that Gnosis (from the Greek word *gnosis,* 'knowledge') is an absolute knowledge which in itself saves, or that Gnosticism is the theory that salvation is obtained by knowledge. But this definition, true and central as it may be, remains inadequate." Puech, therefore, approaches an understanding of this attitude through an exploration of the Gnostic's stance toward time, a strategy that also proves useful for comprehending Percy's relation to this enduring mode of thought.

Puech argues that a Gnostic view of time remains distinct from that of both Hellenism and Christianity. For the Greeks, as I discussed in Chapter 1, time was conceived "above all as cyclical or circular, returning perpetually upon itself, self-enclosed." Because of this emphasis on eternal return, the Greeks developed two sentiments toward time: they either admired the beauty and order of the cosmos, in which everything finds its place, or they grew weary of the "monotonous [and] crushing" repetition. This latter view is, of course, the sentiment of the Stoa.[8]

But the stress on the eternal return had another effect as well. History held little interest for the Greeks. They were unconcerned with the particular and singular. It was the immutable world of form, the general or the ideal, that concerned them. Although continuity exists between the particular and the general—the former participates in the latter and thus establishes a relation between the temporal and the atemporal orders—the particular carries little significance in itself. Furthermore, because a circle is without beginning, middle, or end—and because any point on a circle can be taken indifferently as beginning, middle, or end—the Greeks possessed no "central reference point by which to define and orient a historical past and future." Events in time, then, eternally repeat a cosmic pattern that elicits awe or boredom, two sentiments Kierkegaard would later pronounce subsumable under his aesthetic category.

If the Greeks placed little value on events in time, then Christianity founds itself on a unique historical event. Time is not cyclical; rather, it is linear, "finite at its two extremities, having a beginning and an absolute end." Events in time do not eternally recur. They are irreversible. As a result, life in time becomes full of significance. An individual's passage

---

8. Puech, "Gnosis and Time," in *Man and Time,* 55, 39–40, 45.

through time bears the utmost meaning. The past is gathered up into the present and both point to a fixed end in the future. The future, in turn, gives direction to the past: "Whether near or far, the eschatological end orients the past toward the future and binds the two together in such a way as to make the unilateral direction of time a certainty."[9] In other words, the end gives shape, direction, and meaning to the beginning—the beginning finds its source in the end—and the end is prefigured in the beginning. Unlike the Greek notion of time, the Christian view posits a beginning and end that are both distinct and united. At opposite poles of the line, the beginning and the end are wholly separate yet wholly connected by the line, which is history. Christians await the end of time to discover meaning, yet even as they wait they draw meaning from the end to determine present action. They stand between what already fills time but has not yet reached the fullness to come. The parallels between primitive Christianity's view of time and Kierkegaard's category of repetition seem clear. Both acknowledge *inter esse* as the genuine human placement.

The Gnostic attitude toward time is neither historical nor cosmic, neither a straight line nor a circle. Instead, Puech argues, it is best viewed as a "broken line." Whereas Hellenism proffers a continuity between the temporal and the atemporal, and Christianity posits a movement in and toward fullness, Gnosticism proposes a radical bifurcation between the temporal and the atemporal, between fullness and history. The Gnostic view is primarily dualistic. Because time partakes of the material and visible world, and because this world was created by a "feeble, narrow-minded if not ignorant" god, it has no relation to the invisible and spiritual domain that is truth. The Greek either stands in awe of time or grows weary of it, and the Christian waits in eager anticipation, but the Gnostic "condemns, rejects, [and] rebels." Time is, "in the last analysis, a lie."

Puech notes that in one gnostic system "time was born from the *hysterema*, a *defectus* or *defectio*, a *labes*—a deficiency, error, or fault—from the collapse and dispersion in the void . . . of a reality which had previously existed one and integral, within the pleroma [the original fullness]."[10] That

9. *Ibid.*, 43, 46, 51–52.

10. *Ibid.*, 40, 59, 60, 61, 66. See also Justo L. Gonzales, *A History of Christian Thought* (3 vols.; Nashville, 1970), I, 131.

hysterema and *labes* derive from the same words that describe female reproductive organs indicates the radical and generative evil that pervades the sexual act for some Gnostics (others were extremely licentious), an act that only continues our defective, evil life in time.

The Greek *hystera* means "uterus or womb," but *hysteresis* means "a deficiency"; *labes* shares the same root, *labi,* which in Latin can mean both "to slip, to fall," as in *labile,* and "a lip, or lip-like organ," as in *labium.* Although these etymological connections are my own and not Puech's, they seem to be implied in Puech's later comments on sexuality and the Gnostics. They also find corroboration in Harold Bloom's lucid analysis of Ann Lee, the foundress of the Shakers:

> Ann Lee began as a desperate, lower-class English wife, who had gone through four painful births, lost all four infants, joined a band of Shaking Quakers (in dissent from the main body of Quakers), and was imprisoned for disturbing the peace in Manchester during the summer of 1770. *With waking eyes, she beheld Adam and Eve in the initial act of human sexuality and suddenly understood that lovemaking itself constituted the Fall from Paradise.* By 1774, Ann Lee had removed herself and her followers to America. She died in 1784, only about forty-eight years old, leaving her movement as one of the oddest spiritual legacies in our troubled religious history.[11]

The story of Ann Lee finds its place in Bloom's larger contention that, in its roots, the American religion is not Christian but Gnostic, an insight I will draw on as I explore Eric Voegelin's contribution to understanding "modern Gnosticism" and its relation to Percy's works.

For the Gnostics the perpetual cycle of a generation that is a degeneration (a creation that is a fall, or a birth-into-death and a death-in-life) is recapitulated in even the smallest unit of time. Each moment "arises only to be engulfed in the next moment, in which all things appear, disappear, and reappear in a twinkling." Time is hell, the region where one's "capacity for seeing and hearing is 'narrow,' limited to what is purely actual and close at hand."

Given such a view of time, its extreme dualism and its preoccupation with evil, it is no wonder that Gnosticism proposes an atemporal salvation.

---

11. Harold Bloom, *The American Religion: The Emergence of the Post-Christian Nation* (New York, 1992), 66 (my emphasis).

Salvation, in fact, liberates the Gnostic from time. It sets free the "spiritual" or "perfect" man from the bonds of time. Instead of displaying the fullness of time, salvation "shatters time" and "destroy[s] the world."[12] The Gnostic seeks a return to a lost home, a perfect realm beyond or before the world in which "his substance was pure of all mixture or adulteration." Gnosis provides the vehicle for such liberation.

For the "perfect man" entombed in defective matter, gnosis provides an "absolute Truth, a total Knowledge, in which all the riddles raised by the existence of evil are solved." Through this exhaustive knowledge, the Gnostic answers the triple question: "Who am I and where am I? Whence have I come and why have I come hither? Whither am I going?" What begins as a knowledge for freeing the spiritual self enchained in deficient time ends in a total "mythological" knowledge. Gnosis not only yields the answers to the individual's origins and destiny, but it provides an atemporal "knowledge of the whole universe, visible and invisible, of the structure and development of the divine as well as the physical world. Some of the Gnostics actually call it a total 'science'—in the positive sense of the word— . . . an exhaustive and purely rational explanation of all things." Through gnosis, the Gnostic enters into an elite group, either "a class of *gnostikoi*, 'knowers,' or of *pneumatikoi*, 'spiritual men.' " He thus surpasses time and reenters his "primitive, permanent state" in the total and closed "articulated atemporality" that gnosis supplies.[13]

This "articulated atemporality" provided by the "science" of gnosis sounds very similar to Percy's reflections on "theory." The passage I cited above from "The Loss of the Creature," for example, corresponds closely to the total, atemporal gnosis Puech describes. Like the Gnostics, modern Western civilization turns to "positive science" for knowledge of the self and the world. While the Western world heralds the "sacredness and dignity of the individual," its "idolatry" of science nevertheless fosters a posture that devalues both the world and the individual creatures in it. A scientific attitude precludes the possibility of "seeing" a single entity because it places

12. Puech, "Gnosis and Time," in *Man and Time,* 66, 70; Bloom, *The American Religion,* 50–51.

13. Puech, "Gnosis and Time," in *Man and Time,* 73–75, 54, 76, 84; see also Hans Jonas, *The Gnostic Religion* (Boston, 1958), 32.

theory before it. In a "theorist-consumer" age, another variant of Percy's transcendent-immanent dialectic, neither theorist nor consumer concerns himself with individuals. Percy writes: "The scientific method is correct as far as it goes, but the theoretical mindset, which assigns significance to single things and events only insofar as they are exemplars of theory or items for consumption, is in fact an inflation of a method of knowing to a totalitarian worldview and is unwarranted."[14] The world is quite literally lost in theory. Because it is more tractable than life in time, theory supplants that life with its own "articulated atemporality." Time is nullified, and the world is surpassed in the transcendence of the scientific posture. Furthermore, Percy argues that this "loss of the creature" sets up a radical dualism between experts and consumers. Experts know and plan, while consumers need and experience. The consumer's most exalted moment, itself desperate, comes when he wholly matches his very self to the expert's theory:

> There is the neurotic who asks nothing more of his doctor than that his symptom should prove interesting. When all else fails, the poor fellow has nothing to offer but his own neurosis. But even this is sufficient if only the doctor will show interest when he says, "Last night I had a curious sort of dream; perhaps it will be significant to one who knows about such things. It seems I was standing in a sort of alley—" (I have nothing else to offer you but my own unhappiness. Please say that it, at least, measures up, that it is a *proper* sort of unhappiness.) (*MB*, 56)

Such a posture suggests, paradoxically, that the "true" self of the consumer has nothing to do with time and matter. I say paradoxically because by definition the consumer partakes of the world's goods. But the consumer's surrender to the expert suggests that the true self is located somewhere outside the world and time, *i.e.,* in the theory that the expert holds. Seeing itself as deficient, the material self of the consumer flees to its "true," theoretical self in the hope of gaining approval from the ones who presumably know all about him, the *gnostikoi*.

This reading of Percy's essay gains more credibility when placed in the context of Harold Bloom's understanding of gnosis. Bloom likens Gnosticism to an information theory: "Matter and energy are rejected, or at least

14. Walker Percy, "Why Are You a Catholic?: The Late Novelist's Parting Reflections," *Crisis,* (September, 1990), 18.

placed under the sign of negation. Information becomes the enabler of salvation; the false Creation-Fall concerned matter and energy, but the Pleroma, or Fullness, the original Abyss, is all information."[15] Consumers,
then, place themselves in the hands of those who have information, the
high priests of the pleroma. Salvation will be theirs if they can but educate
themselves, make "informed choices," and so participate in the elite club of
knowers. Percy's diagram of the "lay reader of Freud" in "A Semiotic Primer of the Self" closely parallels Bloom's view of Gnosticism (see *LC,* 118).
The lay reader leaves the world to enter Freud's orbit. But while Freud
managed to maintain a more or less steady orbit, the lay reader cannot sustain his transcendence and so suffers from a "decayed orbit." The lay reader
makes only a temporary entrance into the fullness of information; he is
obliged to reenter the world. As a supreme knower, Freud was not so
obliged.

It should also be noted that the extreme dualistic posture of the Gnostics reflects the Cartesian dualism that Percy once identified as "responsible
for all our evils" (*Con,* 247). In the Jefferson Lecture of 1989, his final public
lecture, Percy chides the humanistic sciences for ignoring the bifurcation set
up in their own methods. Much of this lecture concerns itself with the
chasm between "mind" and "matter" (Descartes' *res cogitans* and *res extensa*).
Percy argues that such a rift "is not in principle closable—that is, not by the
present regnant principles" of the sciences as they are now practiced (*Signposts,* 274). Percy himself does not make the connection between Cartesian
and Gnostic thought, but the parallels seem nevertheless evident. Mind (the
transcendent sphere) is enchained in matter (the immanent sphere) from
which it either continually struggles to flee or in which it becomes totally
absorbed and thus forgets any possibility of transcendence. The "fateful
rift" that forms the "San Andreas Fault in the Modern Mind," mirrors not
only the "three-hundred-year-old dualism" that began with Descartes but
also the Gnostic attitude that has persisted since ancient times and that now
pervades our modern era, especially in the United States, thanks in large
part to Descartes (*Signposts,* 274). Percy noted de Tocqueville's comment
about Descartes in the Jefferson Lecture: "Could it be true, by the way,

15. Bloom, *The American Religion,* 30.

what Tocqueville said of Americans years ago: that Americans are natural-born Cartesians without having read a word of Descartes?" (*Signposts,* 274).

While I will explore the relation between gnosis and Percy's work in more detail below, especially with regard to a "method of knowing" that is inflated "to a totalitarian worldview," I want first to examine briefly some aspects of the primitive Gnostic attitude that have been transformed in the modern era. For this task I turn to not just Harold Bloom but to Eric Voegelin as well, both of whom complement Puech's lucid reflections. It should be noted from the outset, however, that Voegelin and Bloom adopt different attitudes in their analyses. Whereas Voegelin regrets and cautions against the pervasive Gnosticism of modern culture, a stance similar to Percy's, Bloom neither castigates nor celebrates it.

A self-proclaimed "Gnostic Jew," Bloom looks for the "irreducibly religious" element in experience—be it of " 'the divine' or 'the transcendental' or simply 'the spiritual' "—and he argues convincingly that, in America, that element is essentially Gnostic. Bloom goes on to say that "the most Gnostic element in the American Religion is an astonishing reversal of ancient Gnosticism: we worship the Demiurge as God. . . . As for the alien God of the Gnostics, he has vanished." In primitive Gnostic systems, the Demiurge was the creator of the material world, the "ignoramus" who, far removed from the true, totally other God, established the cosmos and time. That this lesser god now receives our veneration signals a movement away from the absolute transcendence of primitive Gnosticism. The Gnostic still flees time and the world, but he flies not so much into the primordial Abyss of the alien God as into the isolated self: "The American finds God in herself or himself, but only after finding the freedom to know God by experiencing a total inward solitude." The self thus sealed within itself tries to escape the contamination of time.

Voegelin points to another reversal that manifests itself in the modern Gnostic attitude. While he argues that the essential thrust of the modern Gnostic impulse retains its emphasis on salvation through knowledge, he suggests a new development in the Gnostic's attitude toward the world. Like Bloom, Voegelin notes a "recession from transcendence": "Gnostic speculation overcame the uncertainty of faith by receding from transcendence and endowing man and his intramundane range of action with the meaning of eschatological fulfillment. In the measure in which this immanentization progressed experientially, civilizational activity became a mystical work of self-salvation. The spiritual strength of the soul which in Christianity was devoted to the sanctification of life could now be diverted into the more appealing, more tangible, and above all, much easier creation of the terrestrial paradise."[16] For Voegelin modern manifestations of gnosis do not disentangle one from a defective world; instead, they are applied to this world in the hopes of correcting it. Thus, Voegelin does not explore so much the Gnostic *self* as he does the *collective* nature of modern Gnosticism and its attempt to create a terrestrial paradise. Like Bloom, Voegelin suggests that Western civilization has forgotten the alien God and worships the Demiurge. Salvation occurs in a perfected time. However, the evil that the primitive Gnostic saw as inevitably bound to the material world is now considered remediable through *collective* civilizational activity in time. Bloom presents the vital expressions of this transformation, but Voegelin displays the morbid ones. For Voegelin, as for Percy, a collective activity based on gnosis leads to a "totalitarian worldview" that stands as a corrective to the "impurities" of life. Attempts to create such a total vision lead to the annihilation of those who cannot be subsumed by the vision. In the twentieth century, of course, the overt impulse to create a society based on gnosis found its most obvious manifestation in Nazi Germany.

Like Voegelin, Percy cautions against such an unrestrained gnosis. Yet like Bloom, he contends that it is all we have. But whereas Bloom asks us simply to "face the fact" that we are Gnostics, Percy looks for another possibility.[17] He offers no programmatic anodyne for an escape from our Gnostic flight. Programs are often themselves part of the problem. Instead he diagnoses and names the predicament. It is significant that *diagnose* (from *dia,* "through, between" and *gignōskein,* "to know") contains the root form of *gnosis.*[18] The word, then, points to Percy's (and Bloom's) contention that one must begin where we are—in the midst of a Gnostic society. However, while Bloom suggests that we look for salvation *through* atem-

---

16. *Ibid.,* 28, 32; Eric Voegelin, *Science, Politics and Gnosticism* (Chicago, 1968); Eric Voegelin, *The New Science of Politics* (Chicago, 1952), 129.

17. Bloom, *The American Religion,* 49.

18. The etymology is taken from *Webster's New Universal Unabridged Dictionary,* 2nd edition.

poral knowledge, Percy argues that the road to salvation lies *between* knowledge and time. The category of "news," as Percy develops it in the "The Message in the Bottle," displays this state of "being between," the *inter esse* of repetition, the posture of the autobiographer.

In this "parable" about islands and castaways, Percy develops a distinction between "news" and "knowledge." He defines a "piece of knowledge" as "knowledge *sub specie aeternitatis*, . . . [which means a] knowledge which can be arrived at anywhere by anyone and at any time" (*MB*, 125). It derives from the objective-empirical, scientific posture that for Percy, following Kierkegaard, falls into the aesthetic sphere. Indifferent to time and place, pieces of knowledge are subject to verification and confirmation by anyone, on any island: "Water boils at 100 degrees at sea level"; "Being comprises essence and existence." A piece of news, on the other hand, "express[es] a contingent and nonrecurring event or state of affairs which event or state of affairs is peculiarly relevant to the concrete predicament of the hearer of the news." Although a type of knowledge, news "cannot possibly be arrived at by any effort of experimentation or reflection or artistic insight." Instead, news is "strictly relevant to the predicament in which the hearer of the news finds himself" (126–27). News, then, is determined by the hearer's posture in time and place.

For people who adopt the scientific, objective-empirical posture, news is irrelevant because they stand outside and above the world as "knower[s] and teller[s]." They do not recognize themselves as being in a predicament in time and place. At best, Percy argues, news items heard from this posture "occupy the very lowest rung of scientific significance: they are particular instances from which hypotheses and theories are drawn" (128). The posture of the castaway (another word for *homo viator*), however, manifests the interest that makes news items relevant. Neither scientist nor complacent consumer, the castaway hears news because he finds himself in a predicament, somewhere between being "at home" and "homeless": "To be a castaway is to be in a grave predicament and this is not a happy state of affairs. But it is very much happier than being a castaway and pretending one is not. This is despair. The worst of all despairs is to imagine one is at home when one is really homeless" (144). The castaway longs, waits, and searches for news that speaks of this grave predicament, a message occluded by the culturally dominant postures of the scientist and consumer.

Percy goes on to make a further distinction between "island news" (akin to knowledge because it is "relevant to the everyday life of any islander on any island at any time") and "news from across the seas," which speaks uniquely to the castaway by addressing his deepest longings. Like knowledge, island news is in the sphere of the immanent, but news from across the seas is "in the sphere of transcendence and is therefore paradoxical" (143, 147). The castaway is "he who waits for news from across the seas" (146). As news, such a message requires a message bearer. It involves an act of communication between one person and another. But the message and the message bearer are not to be accepted uncritically. The castaway accepts the message, first, because he is in a predicament, and the news bearer's words are relevant to it. Secondly, "simply by the gravity of his message," the news bearer displays the authority to speak, and so the castaway should listen to him. Thirdly, the message bearer must speak in "perfect sobriety and in good faith" (147–48).

Although Percy never refers explicitly to Gnosticism in this remarkable essay, his diagnosis of a society and its denizens for whom the relevance of news has been annulled suggests an implicit critique of the Gnostic stance. A society founded on knowledge cannot hear of or see the very predicament it longs to annul. Island news and knowledge *sub specie aeternitatis* "immanentize" the eschaton through their promise of salvation. They are forms of what Bloom classifies as gnosis—information. Percy does not suggest that the castaway ignore such information. On the contrary, it is valuable for day-to-day island existence. But when society and the individual consciousness are such that information seems the only avenue toward salvation, both fall prey to the temptation of self-salvation. On the personal level such a stance deludes one into believing that he is "at home," that he knows the "whole story" of himself, something, as we have seen in the discussion of autobiography, one can never know. At the level of history it fosters a "totalitarian" view that eliminates differences in the name of purity. The castaway rejects these self-enclosed island salvations and awaits the news that speaks of his true homelessness.

While Percy's works—both novels and essays—are a form of island news and not news from across the seas, they nevertheless try to reestablish in his characters and in the reader a posture whereby news from across the seas would again be relevant. His "diagnosis" of the modern malaise suggests a "treatment" that stands between knowledge and time. For Percy, as for Kierkegaard, such a stance finds its truest expression in the "news" of faith, a form of knowledge that redeems time. Since he sees himself as "without authority" to deliver news from across the seas, however, he writes his island news so that he might at least name the ultimate despair of life lived in the purely aesthetic sphere.[19]

The epigraphs to "The Message in the Bottle," one from Thomas Aquinas and the other from Kierkegaard, suggest from the start Percy's category of "news":

> The act of faith consists essentially in knowledge and there we find its formal or specific perfection. (Aquinas, *De Veritate*)

> Faith is not a form of knowledge; for all knowledge is either knowledge of the eternal, excluding the temporal and the historical as indifferent, or it is pure historical knowledge. No knowledge can have for its object the absurdity that the eternal is the historical. (Kierkegaard, *Philosophical Fragments*)

Percy comments on this juxtapositioning of epigraphs in an interview with Jan Nordby Gretlund:

> Well, it is a classical dispute between Catholics and Protestants whether faith is a form of knowledge. I thought it was a very nice opposition to have Kierkegaard making a clear statement that faith *is not* a form of knowledge, it is a leap onto [sic] the absurd. St. Thomas Aquinas saying in his classical thirteenth-century way that faith *is* a form of knowledge. It is different from scientific knowing, but it is a form of knowledge. I tend to agree with Aquinas there, even though I am more sympathetic with Kierkegaard. I am on his wavelength, I understand his phenomenology, his analysis of the existential predicament of modern man. Aquinas did not have that, but I think Aquinas was right about faith. It is not a leap into the absurd, it is an act of faith, which is a form of knowledge." (*Con*, 204)

The emphasis on action once again signals the concern and interest that pervade Percy's works.

Percy, then, does not offer yet another call—"Come!"—that would annul the difficulties of life in time. He does not offer knowledge *sub specie*

---

19. Percy's reference to "writing without authority" relates to Kierkegaard's "The Difference Between a Genius and an Apostle," an essay Percy once described as being "tremendously important" to him (*Con*, 113).

aeternitatis, an "articulated atemporality," that promises salvation. Rather, in a society where gnosis reigns unrestrained, where "everyone is an apostle of sorts, ringing doorbells and bidding his neighbor to believe this and do that. In such times, when everyone is saying 'Come!' when radio and television say nothing else but 'Come!' it may be that the best way to say 'Come!' is to remain silent. Sometimes silence itself is a 'Come!' " (*MB,* 148). Percy's works find a good measure of expression in what they do not say. This silence questions the presumed closure and wholeness of a Gnostic culture and allows for the possibility of repetition. The "gaps" in *The Moviegoer* and *The Last Gentleman,* as I tried to show in the last chapter, provide openings for the possibility of this "silent speaking." And in the silence that inevitably follows an end, after characters have made their decisions and after readers have read the last word, the possibility for a new beginning manifests itself.[20]

Lewis Lawson's essay, "Walker Percy's Silent Character," makes this point abundantly clear in the context of *Lancelot.* Lawson shows how Father John, ostensibly a mere receptacle for the ranting of Lancelot Lamar in his prison cell, actually occupies a central place in the novel by means of his silence: "The priest has tried to tell Lance something by his silence throughout their five days together and is telling him once again by his decision to minister in Alabama. . . . Father John has stood there those five days then as a silent invitation, as a character who could be no more eloquent, and Lance, knowing what the silence says, has fought to protect himself by his noise. The next step is up to Lance."[21] Lawson could just as well have said that the next step is up to the reader. For Percy also wants the reader to decide in the silence that follows this ending. Will the reader accept the self-actualized apocalypse and renewal of Lance—the logical end of his radically Gnostic vision—or will he choose the silent "Come!" of Father John? Like Lance, the reader is left in silence. In his interview with Jan Nordby Gretlund, Percy suggests that he wants the reader to decide: "What I was doing was to try to destroy the middle ground. . . . At the end of *Lancelot* I was

---

20. For more on "silence," see Schleifer and Markley, eds., *Kierkegaard and Literature,* 5; Pat Bigelow, *Kierkegaard and the Problem of Writing* (Tallahassee, 1987); and *Con,* 235.

21. Lawson, *Following Percy,* 178–95.

trying to present two radical points of view, neither of which is accepted by most people, most Americans" (*Con,* 209, 211).

Percy's anti-Gnostic stance, then, is less articulated than it is suggested. Although there is mention of the "peculiar gnosis of trains" in *The Moviegoer,* and Tom More is described as a victim of "gnostic pride" in *Love in the Ruins,* these are, as Cleanth Brooks points out, the sole references to Gnosticism in Percy's works.[22] Percy even commented once that he "hadn't thought of gnosticism" when he wrote *Lancelot* (*Con,* 211). Yet as Lawson's "Gnosis and Time in *Lancelot*" reveals, there are direct parallels between this, the darkest of Percy's novels, and the analysis of Gnostic time provided by Puech. Lance's "narrow view" from his cell, for example, only grants truth to "what is at hand," as does the disjointed time of the black-and-white videotaped "movies" Lance has made for material evidence of the crime that involves, in his skewed view, pure materiality—his wife's sexual infidelity. In every turn of the novel, especially in the climactic explosion of Belle Isle Plantation, Lance tries to "shatter time" by projecting gnosis for the eradication of sexual evil. He even plays on the Gnostic compulsion for knowledge when he tells Father John: "I had to know. If Merlin [a movie director] 'knew' my wife, I had to know his knowing her" (*L,* 90). Lance knows the end of his story (and history) because he will himself bring it about. He wants "the whole picture" (97). Lawson also shows how Lance's three-tiered view of sexual history corresponds to Voegelin's analysis of similar Gnostic visions of history, beginning with Joachim of Fiore and continuing in Hitler's view of the Third Reich. Father John's silence counters Lance's delusions of wholeness. Like the autobiographer, Father John knows only that he cannot know the whole story. He thus enters the ordinary everyday. He will go to Alabama, not to await the closure of history in Lance's Third Revolution, but to "turn bread into flesh, forgive the sins of Buick dealers, administer communion to suburban housewives" (277).

In one way or another, all of Percy's main characters move out of a Gnostic attitude into the openness of repetition. Binx abandons his vertical search—the scientific search that annuls time—in favor of the horizontal search in time. Will Barrett, who hopes to engineer his life according to the

22. Brooks, "Walker Percy and Modern Gnosticism," in *The Art of Walker Percy,* ed., Broughton, 260.

scientific principles of psychoanalysis, longs for the news that would speak of his alienation. In the same novel Sutter Vaught expresses the licentiousness characteristic of some Gnostic sects. Tom More of *Love in the Ruins* hopes to cure the "riven self and the riven world" by means of the ultimate scientific instrument—the lapsometer. At the end of the novel he is "chastened" by Fr. Smith in the confessional, and he returns to a less grandiose life with Ellen. That book also portrays the radical dualism and polarity that are consequences of life in a Gnostic society. In *The Second Coming,* the older Will Barrett contrives a plan that he believes will produce firm knowledge of the existence of God. Barrett receives an answer, but not in the way he had anticipated. And Tom More of *The Thanatos Syndrome* contends with doctors who, in totalitarian fashion, would purify the state of its imperfections. More, however, remains a true psychiatrist, a "doctor of the soul" who, instead of applying Gnostic theory, listens to the individual stories of his patients. *Lancelot,* then, is not the only book in which Percy deals with Gnosticism.[23]

It is interesting to note, however, that whereas Percy's earlier fiction and essays counter the doom of a Gnostic attitude and offer a recovery "silently," his later works deal with it more or less explicitly. This movement from silence to outright portrayal can best be seen, I think, by examining Percy's complicated response to the most overt of Gnostic societies in this "century of death," Nazi Germany.

In one of his letters to Shelby Foote, Percy comments on the strengths and weaknesses of William Styron's *Sophie's Choice:*

> I found not so much bad Faulkner as occasionally crappy cliché: ". . . her graceful undulant walk." He had a lot of nerve taking on the Holocaust and for this I admire him—nobody's been able to handle it, not even the survivors, maybe especially not the survivors. I suspect that it can't be handled, that is, the dead weight and mystery of the horror can't be got hold of by esthetic categories— and when you try, bad things happen, both to the writer and the subject. . . . The only way you can write about such a thing is not to write about it.[24]

23. See also Ted R. Spivey, *The Writer as Shaman: The Pilgrimages of Conrad Aiken and Walker Percy* (Macon, Ga, 1986), 117–21.

24. Walker Percy to Shelby Foote, August 29, 1979, in Percy Papers, SHC.

Percy once commented in an interview the he could never "take on" the Holocaust in his writing (*MCon*, 32). Yet his comment about "not writing" about it can be taken as a reference to his indirect or "silent" treatment of it. I do not mean to suggest that he probes the mystery of the horror by entering the mind of a character who has lived through it. Instead, as numerous writers and thinkers about the Nazi genocide of the Jews have noted, the event is so particular in history that the universalizing of it by means of literature inevitably deforms it.[25] A moral imperative to write nevertheless impresses itself not only upon those who lived through it, but also those who have inherited our "post-Holocaust" civilization, an oxymoron if ever there was one. Writers must "write against the silence," as Berel Lang suggests, with the awareness that their efforts from the start will fall short. This being so, the "canniest writers," as Irving Howe puts it, take on the Holocaust "through strategies of indirection and circuitous narrative that leave untouched the central horror."

Percy, too, leaves the central horror untouched. Yet throughout both his essays and fiction he writes about the conditions he sees as making possible such death-dealing in the first place. He does not probe the central horror because, as Claude Lanzman has written, "between the conditions that permitted extermination and the extermination itself—the *fact* of extermination—there is a break in continuity, a hiatus, an abyss."[26] The abyss itself, Howe continues, "is the essence of the Holocaust." Writing about this abyss demands a "silent" treatment.

It may be useful, then, to trace Percy's early indirection and insight about the conditions that made possible the Nazi genocide of the Jews and then to explore his more direct handling of those conditions in his later writings.[27] In his early essays, "The Loss of the Creature" (1958) and "The Message in the Bottle" (1959), for example, Percy writes about the result of unrestrained gnosis by "not writing about it." In one of his last published essays, however, the one I have already cited from *Crisis*, he makes an overt

25. Berel Lang, ed., *Writing and the Holocaust* (New York, 1988); and Lang, *Act and Idea*.

26. Lang, *Act and Idea*, 150ff.; Irving Howe, "Writing and the Holocaust," in *Writing and the Holocaust*, ed. Lang, 194, 178, quoted by Howe.

27. Howe, "Writing and the Holocaust," in *Writing and the Holocaust*, ed. Lang, 178. The "Nazi genocide of the Jews" is Lang's preferred term for referring to what is more commonly termed the Holocaust.

connection between theory and Nazism: "Marx and Stalin, Nietzsche and Hitler were . . . theorists. When theory is applied, not to matter or beasts, but to man, the consequence is that millions of men can be eliminated without compunction or even much interest. Survivors of both Hitler's holocaust and Stalin's terror reported that their oppressors were not 'horrible' or 'diabolical' but seemed, on the contrary, quite ordinary, even bored by their actions, as if it were all in a day's work."[28] In expository prose one expects a writer to be overt. Yet the shift from indirect and subtle argument to clear refutation seems curious. If the best way to write about the "dead weight and mystery of the horror" that surround even the conditions of the Holocaust is not to write about it, then why does Percy begin writing more directly about it in his later works, especially in *The Thanatos Syndrome?*

In *The Moviegoer* and *The Last Gentleman* there are no conspicuous references to the Holocaust, even though the former contains very strong denunciations of "scientific humanism," especially toward the end. In disgust with himself and his "dark pilgrimage," Binx reflects on "the very century of merde, the great shithouse of scientific humanism where needs are satisfied, everyone becomes an anyone, a warm and creative person" (*MG*, 228). Percy alluded to this denunciation when he delivered his acceptance speech for the National Book Award: "The book attempts a modest restatement of the Judeo-Christian notion that man is more than an organism in an environment, more than an integrated personality, more even than a mature and creative individual, as the phrase goes. He is a wayfarer and a pilgrim" (*Signposts*, 246). And Percy's second novel reveals the only options left in a Gnostic culture—immanence and transcendence—but allows the reader to arrive at his own conclusions about such a bifurcated reality. Percy writes about the Holocaust in these first two novels by "not writing about it." He implies that, in a culture where "everyone becomes an anyone," it becomes very easy to treat others like the "merde" Binx finds around him. In such a culture, people can be disposed of "without much compunction." It is not surprising, then, that as a wayfarer and exile, Binx keeps a keen eye on the Jews: "Ever since Wednesday I have become acutely aware of Jews. There is a clue here, but of what I cannot say." Neither is it surprising that at the moment he rails against the "century of merde," he also "know[s] less than

28. Percy, "Why Are You a Catholic?", 16.

[he] ever knew before," a good sign for someone trapped in the gnosis of contemporary culture.[29]

The dialectic of immanence-transcendence in *The Last Gentleman* points both backward and forward. It restates Binx's wavering between consumer and scientist, and it anticipates "More's Syndrome," the chronic "angelism/ bestialism" that besets the characters of *Love in the Ruins.* Following Pascal (*Qui fait l'ange, fait la bête*) who, in turn, borrows his language from the tradition of the Great Chain of Being, Percy suggests that those who wish to know like the angels inevitably produce some form of bestialism. Hitler's Third Reich followed the flowering of the arts and sciences during the Weimar Republic.

The first overt reference to the Holocaust in Percy's fiction occurs in *Love in the Ruins,* and it alludes to this very point. Tom More reflects: "Once I was commiserating with a patient, an old man, a Jewish refugee from the Nazis—he'd got out with his skin but lost his family to Auschwitz—so I said something conventional against the Germans. The old fellow bristled like a Prussian and put me down hard and spoke of the superiority of German universities, German science, German music, German philosophy. My God, do you suppose the German Jews would have gone along with Hitler if he had let them?" (*LR,* 149). Percy seems to suggest here that angelism/bestialism has struck modern consciousness so deeply that even a victim of its most horrible manifestation can miss its significance.

Of course, not all survivors of the German *Lager* resemble Percy's "Jewish refugee." Primo Levi, for one, recognizes very clearly the Gnostic angelism/bestialism of modern culture, especially as it manifested itself in the German quest for purity. In *The Periodic Table,* for example, Levi (not unlike Percy in that he was a chemist turned writer) continually refers to the antagonism between spirit and matter and in fact makes that theme part of the framework of his exceptional book. At one point, reflecting on the boredom of his chosen career, he writes: "Chemistry, for me, had stopped being . . . a source [of certainty]. It led to the heart of Matter, and Matter was our ally precisely because the Spirit, dear to Fascism, was our enemy; but, having reached the fourth year of Pure Chemistry, I could no longer

29. *MG,* 88, 228. See also Lang, *Act and Idea,* 165ff.

ignore the fact that chemistry itself, or at least that which we were being administered, did not answer my questions."[30] Levi's identification of fascism as "Spirit" corresponds to Percy's comments about theory and a "totalitarian worldview." Just as the spirit of fascism wishes to create *pneumatikoi,* spiritual men inflamed and dedicated to its cause, so theory creates *gnostikoi,* knowers who become founts of pure information, the theory that keeps fascism vital. In either case the impurity of matter ("intractable matter," as Levi calls it at one point) is fallaciously transformed by the purity of theory. Like Percy, Levi wishes to restore some balance to the deficient polarizations that come about in choosing solely spirit or matter.

Elsewhere in *The Periodic Table,* Levi considers the different reactions of zinc in its pure and impure forms to acid. Acid "gulps it down" when impurities are present. Yet zinc "resists the attack" when in its pure form. Levi reflects: "One could draw from this two conflicting philosophical conclusions: the praise of purity, which protects from evil like a coat of mail; the praise of impurity, which gives rise to changes, in other words, to life. I discarded the first, disgustingly moralistic, and I lingered to consider the second, which I found more congenial. In order for the wheel to turn, for life to be lived, impurities are needed. . . . Dissension, diversity, the grain of salt and mustard are needed: Fascism does not want them, forbids them; . . . it wants everybody to be the same." Fascism strives for a Gnostic purity, a condition unstained by time. It wants to subsume differences into the original singularity of the pleroma. It is significant that Levi, like Percy, turns to writing in order to combat and reflect on his immersion in a Gnostic culture. In fact, Levi once wrote that his experience of the *Lager* and his writing about it gave him a "reason for life."[31] Language combats Gnostic purity because it combines elements of matter and spirit, impurity and purity. As triadic behavior, it may be the bridge—as Percy suggests time and again, but most emphatically in the Jefferson Lecture—between the chasm Descartes created when he posited *res extensa* and *res cogitans.* It is no accident that book burnings occur in totalitarian regimes. The angelism/bestialism in Percy's *Love in the Ruins,* then, points to the same antagonism

---

30. Primo Levi, *The Periodic Table,* trans. Raymond Rosenthal (New York, 1984), 52.

31. *Ibid.,* 33, 34; Primo Levi, *The Drowned and the Saved,* trans. Raymond Rosenthal (New York, 1988), 174.

between spirit and matter (purity and impurity) that Levi writes about. The attempt to create a society founded on the pure knowledge provided by More's lapsometer can lead to the bestialism of the German *Lager.*

It is interesting to note that Levi writes both indirectly and directly in his dealing with the Holocaust, and he seems to evince an opposite movement from that of Percy. Levi continually writes against the silence in whatever way he can, but his first books, especially the Dantean trilogy—*Survival in Auschwitz, Moments of Reprieve,* and *The Reawakening*—deal more or less directly with his camp experiences and his return to "ordinary" life. And his later stories and books, *The Periodic Table, The Sixth Day and Other Tales,* deal with that experience more indirectly.[32] In "Angelic Butterfly," for example, Levi constructs the tale of one Dr. Leeb, who lived in an age "conducive to theories" and whose ambition was to tap a "further capacity for development" in man. Dr. Leeb carries out his experiment, but what he creates is not the angels he thought would arise if people "subjected [them]selves to his manipulations," but beasts that "looked like vultures." At the story's end Professor Leeb is believed dead, but the fact remains uncertain. Readers are left with the sobering reflection: "I believe that we haven't heard the last of Professor Leeb."[33]

Here Levi seems to display some of the canniness Howe cites as indicative of the better treatments of the Holocaust in writing. For in this story Levi not only alludes indirectly to the brutal experiments performed by Nazi doctors, but also the angelism/bestialism that besets attempts to immanentize the eschaton through "manipulations." The provocative last line, furthermore, serves as a forewarning of those who would follow Dr. Leeb's path. Like Percy, then, Levi finds circuitous and indirect writing suitable for treating the "dead weight and mystery of the horror."

Percy, however, becomes more direct in his later writings. In *Lancelot* and *The Second Coming,* references to Hitler and the Holocaust become

32. Primo Levi, *Survival in Auschwitz,* trans. Stuart Woolf (New York, 1961); *Moments of Reprieve,* trans. Ruth Feldman (New York, 1987); *The Reawakening,* trans. Stuart Woolf (New York, 1987). For some comments on Levi's trilogy, see Lawrence Langer, "Interpreting Survivor Testimony," in *Writing and the Holocaust,* ed. Lang, 26–40. See also Lang, *Act and Idea,* 125ff.; Primo Levi, *The Sixth Day and Other Tales,* trans. Raymond Rosenthal (New York, 1990).

33. Levi, "Angelic Butterfly," in *The Sixth Day,* 21–25.

more explicit, even though they still occupy a secondary place in the narratives. Lance's ranting against this "age of interest" in which no one is responsible for his actions leads him to search for a "single sin," something conspicuously absent from the twentieth century: "What about Hitler, the gas ovens and so forth? What about them? As everyone knows and says, Hitler was a madman. And it seems nobody else was responsible. Everyone was following orders. It is even possible that there was no such order, that it was all a bureaucratic mistake" (*L,* 138). Even so terrible an event as the Holocaust can be explained away in this aesthetic age. Lance implies that the very possibility of explaining it away itself contributes to its occurrence. When psychological categories are applied ("Hitler was a madman"), no one is responsible. The Gnostic, to recall Puech, bases his freedom on gnosis, even "at the risk of falling into nihilism, anarchism, amoralism, or even licentious immoralism."[34] Such ethical categories become meaningless, however, to an age in the grip of such a liberating knowledge. Lance cannot find sin in Hitler's atrocities because the age will not allow him to. Thus, he will enact his own ethical "order" based on a "stern code, a gentleness toward women and an intolerance of swinishness, a counsel kept and above all a readiness to act." Although he tells Father John that his will be an entirely new order—"Don't confuse it with anything you've heard of before. . . . Don't confuse it with the Nazis"—he, like the Nazis, wants to bring about his own apocalypse and recovery. He destroys time in the name of gnosis in order to bring about the closure of history in a self and a society of his own making.[35]

This Gnostic totality, again, counters the openness of the autobiographical act. Lance's "readiness to act" differs from the concerned-action-in-time posture discussed in Chapter 1 because it places the ideal (a "stern code") before the actual. The present, and thus the future, cannot become for Lance because they already "have been" as an ideal, a romantic "IT," if you will. Like the poet of Kierkegaard's *Repetition,* however, Percy's other protagonists (including Father John) stumble into their ability to act in

34. Puech, "Gnosis and Time," 70.
35. *L,* 157, 156. See Lewis P. Simpson, *The Brazen Face of History: Studies in the Literary Consciousness in America* (Baton Rouge, 1980), 233–54.

time. Their repetitive posture comes to them to the degree that they aban-
don, often unwittingly, this same Gnostic totality and closure.

In *The Second Coming,* Percy returns to the implicit link between scientific humanism and the Holocaust. While he circumscribes the issue in
The Moviegoer—i.e., he writes about it by "not writing about it"—the link
becomes explicit in *The Second Coming.* In large part the novel follows the
older Will Barrett's attempts to come to terms with and place the memory
of his father's death by suicide. Barrett "remembered everything," the narrator tells us (*SC,* 79). Almost anything serves as a signal that fires his memory: a triangular patch of land reminds him of missed opportunities with
Ethel Rosenblum, a high-school classmate and would-be sweetheart, and
the sound of stretching barbed wire announces the hunting trip during
which his father first tried to kill himself and Barrett. In his car Barrett
carries physical reminders of his father—two guns. One is a Greener, the
shotgun with which his father ultimately took his life and that comes to
represent to Barrett his father's "love of death" (148). The other is a Luger,
a pistol his father had taken from an SS colonel and that provides Barrett
clues to the unnamed malaise, the "death-in-life" out of which his father
knew no escape but suicide.

The Luger signals a connection between his father's humanism and the
Holocaust. Recalling the German "colonel's black cap with its Totenkopf
insignia and some pictures" his father had taken along with the Luger, Barrett reflects on his father's stories of World War II:

> Strange that he, my father, often spoke of the Ardennes and the Rhine and
> Weimar but never mentioned Buchenwald, which was only four miles from
> Weimar and which Patton took three weeks later, never mentioned that the
> horrified Patton paraded fifteen hundred of Weimar's best humanistic Germans
> right down the middle of Buchenwald to see the sights. Patton, of all people,
> no Goethe he who said to the fifteen hundred not look you sons of Goethe but
> look you sons of bitches (is not this in fact, Father, where your humanism ends
> in the end?). Yet he, my father, never mentioned that . . . (132)

Even the Faulkneresque rhythms imply what the words make explicit. Humanism is not enough, be it of Barrett's father or of one of Percy's "literary
fathers."[36] Humanism, in fact, leads to the horrors of the *Lager,* for it sig-

---

36. See Allen, *A Southern Wayfarer.*

nals the "recession from transcendence" and the "immanentization of the eschaton" that "collective civilizational activity" enacts. For Percy it leads to the gnosis that "shatters time" by means of "articulated atemporality" (theory), a comprehensive "science" that inflates knowing to a "totalitarian worldview." In the name of such humanism, millions of people can be killed "without compunction or even much interest."

What occupies a rather small place in *The Second Coming*, however, moves to the foreground in Percy's last novel, *The Thanatos Syndrome*. Here the references to the Holocaust and to Germany are explicit and numerous. Although Percy returns to his befuddled Anglo-Saxon psychiatrist-protagonist, Tom More, two other main characters are of obvious German descent: John Van Dorn, referred to throughout the novel simply as "Van Dorn," and Father Smith, whose "Confession" and "Footnote" provide the central anti-Gnostic message of the novel. Germany seems very much on Percy's mind as the book unfolds. Percy himself traveled there in the summer of 1934. But it is the Germany of the Weimar Republic (1919–1933) that finds emphasis in the novel, not that of the National Socialists. The Nazis and the Holocaust do occupy a significant place, but are used mostly as examples. As in *The Second Coming,* they signal the end of an unchecked humanism. The bestialism of the Nazi *Lager* marks the end of Weimar angelism. In the name of atemporal theory that purports to advance humankind, the Weimar scientists lay the groundwork for the rise of a Hitler. As Father Smith tells Tom More:

> If you are a lover of Mankind in the abstract like Walt Whitman, who wished the best for Mankind, you will probably do no harm and might even write good poetry and give pleasure. . . .
>
> . If you are a theorist of Mankind like Rousseau or Skinner, who believes he understands man's brain and in the solitariness of his study or laboratory writes books on the subject, you are also probably harmless and might even contribute to human knowledge. . . .
>
> But if you put the two together, a lover of Mankind and a theorist of Mankind, what you've got now is Robespierre or Stalin or Hitler and the Terror, and millions dead for the good of Mankind. (*TS,* 129)

It was the Weimar doctors who, in the name of the betterment of mankind, allowed the termination of lives "unfit for living." Percy's acknowledgment of Frederic Wertham's "remarkable book," *A Sign for Cain,* in the Prologue to *The Thanatos Syndrome* only amplifies what Father Smith makes explicit about a society in the grip of Gnostic theory.[37]

Wertham's book, subtitled *An Exploration of Human Violence,* contends that one reason for the proliferation of violence in the modern age may be a result of an improper understanding of it. A proper vision eschews the notion that violence is fated or that it is purely accidental in nature: "Looked at superficially, it may appear that there is a lot of inevitability about violence. But the more we concentrate scientifically on a concrete question in the general stream of violence, the more we find that pure coincidence, accident, and chance disappear, and causal sequences of events emerge." Every act of violence, then, has a long history of contributing factors: "Social customs, institutions, theories, and beliefs" all play a role as "violence-fostering factors." The violence unleashed by the Nazis upon the Jews and other "impurities" was not so much a "freak" accident of history as it was a logical end of modes of thought that had preceded it. Although Hitler provided the impetus for its enactment, the Holocaust had its roots in the scientism and research begun during the Weimar Republic, especially with the publication in 1920 of *The Release of the Destruction of Life Devoid of Value,* a proto-euthanasia manual. Wertham writes: "The book advocated that the killing of 'worthless people' be released from penalty and legally permitted. It was written by two prominent scientists, the jurist Karl Binding and the psychiatrist Alfred Hoche. The concept of 'life devoid of value' or 'life not worth living' was not a Nazi invention, as is often thought. It derives from this book."[38] Once the question of the "value of life" reaches the floor, Wertham argues, a plethora of "legitimated" violence follows.

In *The Thanatos Syndrome,* Father Smith refers directly to this book in his "confession." It was given to him by one of the doctors he met during his trip to Germany in the 1930s, and it created a "heated argument" in the scientific community he came to know: "[The argument] seemed to be between those who believed in the elimination of people who were useless, useless to anyone, to themselves, the state, and those who believed in eu-

37. Frederic Wertham, *A Sign for Cain: An Exploration of Human Violence* (New York, 1966).

38. *Ibid.,* 22, 43–44, 161; Karl Binding and Alfred Hoche, *The Release of the Destruction of Life Devoid of Value* (Leipzig, 1920).

thanasia only for those who suffered from hopeless diseases or defects. . . . I must confess to you that I didn't warm up to those fellows, distinguished as they were. But I must also confess that I was not repelled by their theories and practice of eugenics" (*TS*, 246–47). Here Father Smith confesses his attraction to the Gnostic theory that eliminates the impure in the name of purity. This confession foreshadows the more emphatic one he makes at the end of his discourse, that he would have joined his friend who entered the *Schutzstaffel* had he been a German and not an American: "I would have gone to the Junkerschule, sworn the solemn oath of the Teutonic knights at Marienberg, and joined the Schutzstaffel. Listen. Do you hear me? *I would have joined him*" (248–49, Percy's emphasis).

The confession of his attraction to the theory of eugenics reflects an intellectual assent to gnosis, but his desire to enter the SS signals a volitional assent. In his interview with Jan Nordby Gretlund, Percy, following Gabriel Marcel, comments on the positive aspects of mass movements: "Marcel . . . had the nerve to say [that] we tend to overlook something positive about the mass movements. It is easy to say how wrong they were. It is easy to overlook the positive things: the great sense of verve and vitality. This I was very much aware of in Germany in 1934" (*Con*, 208). Percy in no way condones the actions of the Nazi regime; he is well aware of the "dead weight and mystery of the horror" that the Nazis perpetrated on those they considered unfit for life in the Third Reich. Yet he also recognizes the appeal of mass movements to an age that proclaims the self autonomous. In such an age the self becomes ever more isolated and thus longs for a sense of commonality of purpose that would relieve it of loneliness. Like war and sex, mass movements provide such a common purpose. They provide avenues for the self to feel part of something beyond itself.

It is noteworthy, then, that Father Smith "confesses" to Tom More. The word *confess* derives from the Latin prefix *com*, "together," and *fateri*, "to acknowledge." Father Smith did not ultimately join the SS; rather, together with Tom, he acknowledges his attraction to them. He breaks the isolation of the self in his confession, through his speaking to another person, not through the violence of war or through another mass movement. Wertham writes that "communication is the opposite of violence. Where communication ends, violence begins."[39] Like St. Augustine, then, Father

39. Wertham, *A Sign for Cain*, 50.

Smith confesses his sins, and in so doing he confesses the life he has chosen over the death of a possibly violent past. When Tom asks him why he became a priest, Father Smith responds:

> "What else?"
> "What else what?"
> "That's all."
> He shrugs, appearing to lose interest. "In the end one must choose—given the chance."
> "Choose what?"
> "Life or death. What else?" (*TS*, 257)

Father Smith chooses and confesses life over the death of Gnostic certainty. When he asks Tom, "Do you think we're any different from the Germans?" he suggests a parallel between the Nazis and the projects undertaken by Van Dorn and the other well-meaning scientists in the novel. Such projects based on "angelic" knowledge have already led to the bestialism of child molestation at Belle Ame Academy. But Father Smith suggests that the "qualitarian centers" that euthanize people unfit for life and the Blue Boy project that eliminates social problems through mixing heavy sodium ions with drinking water mark the beginnings of a gnosis that will end in the gas chambers—*thanatos*. At one point in the novel Tom More tells his colleagues the reason for Father Smith's refusal to support their endeavors: "He thinks you'll end by killing Jews" (351).

In Percy's last work of fiction, then, he launches a frontal attack on the gnosis of scientific humanism. The question remains, however, why change tactics from indirect to direct confrontation? Why write explicitly about the "dead weight and mystery of the horror" now, when in 1979 Percy argued that the best way to write about it was "not to write about it," to deal with it silently?

It seems to me that three responses could be set forth, each related to the views of time outlined earlier in the chapter. On the one hand, the change in tactic reflects a movement similar to the linearity of time as viewed in the Christian perspective. *The Thanatos Syndrome* stands at the end as the fulfillment of what Percy has been writing about all along. This last novel reflects the "either/or" that Percy writes about throughout his career, the choice between *eros* or *thanatos,* and the novels along the way find their source in them. Each novel, furthermore, "repeats" this end in its unique fashion. Percy writes about the same thing all along, but his themes find their ultimate fulfillment in his last work. Another perspective might be compared to the circularity of the Greek version of time. Percy says all he has to say in the beginning, in *The Moviegoer,* and then repeats in his other novels what has been established as the "ideal" in that novel. The later novels are lesser incarnations of this first, primordial one. Still another view could be likened to the Gnostic's view of time. Percy radically breaks from his earlier "silent" treatment of the Holocaust and embarks on an overt refutation of the gnosis that leads to it. In this perspective, *The Thanatos Syndrome* stands alone as an "alien" amidst Percy's other works. This alien character relates to the confessional quality of the novel, the "acknowledgment together" by author and character of their attraction to the Gnosticism against which they rail. I mean to say that Percy breaks with his commitment of "not writing about the Holocaust" in order to deal with (and ultimately condemn) his own attraction to the vitality of German life that he experienced during his trip in 1934.

In an interview with Phil McCombs, Percy once admitted that although his experiences in Germany were nowhere near "so dramatic as Father Smith's," he nevertheless transformed them in composing *The Thanatos Syndrome.* Like Father Smith, Percy stayed with a family whose son "was dead serious. . . . [He was] graduating from the Hitler Jugend and going into the Schutzstaffel." And just as Father Smith was impressed by the young man he befriended, Percy admits that "this youth was the one who made an impression on me." There can be little doubt, then, that Percy uses Father Smith as a mouthpiece for his own views against the scientific humanism that seeks to engineer society in the name of "doing good." Furthermore, Percy's comments to Gretlund indicate that, like Father Smith, he was profoundly attracted to the verve that pervaded Germany during Hitler's rise to power. Jay Tolson cites a comment by Shelby Foote regarding this trip: "[Walker] was tremendously impressed by what he saw there. Tremendously impressed." Tolson goes on to argue that character and writer coalesce in the pages of *The Thanatos Syndrome,* especially in the reflections on Germany. He suggests that what so impressed the young Percy, whose "cynicism could verge on nihilism," was the "sense of purpose of the true-believing Nazi." It is not unreasonable to propose, then, that

Father Smith's confession is also Walker Percy's confession. Often preoccupied by "troubling questions about life's meaning," Percy found himself
deeply impressed and attracted to the resolve "unto death" of the National
Socialists. When Father Smith says that he "would have joined" his friend,
Percy himself seems not too far behind the persona.[40]

If *The Thanatos Syndrome* is viewed as an "alien," then, its difference
derives from the alien within Percy himself, that "other" who surfaces and
finds expression in the character of Father Smith. In his previous novels,
the other seems to be projected onto the culture at large. In this final one,
he quarrels with himself. While it is no doubt true that his earlier works
also evince this quarrel with himself, the overt, confessional quality of *The
Thanatos Syndrome* suggests that Percy's inner struggle with Gnosticism had
at last surfaced. The movement from indirect to direct confrontation signals
a deeper willingness on Percy's part to acknowledge with his reader that he
is himself a product of the very culture he castigates, this "century of death."

His diagnosis of our Gnostic culture, then, stands not only between
time and knowledge, but also between (*inter esse*) the "unwarranted totalitarian view" and the sense of purpose (concern) that such a view provides.
He condemns the totalitarian view while at the same time standing in awe
of its power to give direction to an otherwise formless life. Percy's works
ultimately reject the self-actualized and self-contained closure of history that
a Gnostic apocalypse and recovery would supply, and they point to that
repetition that provides a sense of purpose without positing an absolute
knowledge of an end. Just as the autobiographer confesses what *has been* in
order to clear a space for and inhabit what *now becomes,* so Percy acknowledges with his reader that life, which has been all along, but that has been
deprived of significance, now becomes possible in the telling itself. Percy
de-structs a totalized Gnostic vision of life so that a recovery and openness
might emerge. Apocalypse implies recovery; an end offers a new beginning.
However, neither can be encompassed by the articulated atemporality that
is theory. In his final works, Percy breaks his silence only to confess. And
the confession of a life, of course, is one of the sources of modern autobiography.

40. Phil McCombs, "Century of Thanatos: Walker Percy and His 'Subversive Message,' " *Southern Review,* n.s., XXIV (1988), 809, rpt. in *MCon,* 189–207; Tolson, *Pilgrim in the
Ruins,* 115, 118, 113.

4

Repetition and *Graphein:* Metaphor and the Mystery of Language and Narrative

Shakespeare had it easy: he had the language, a new language busting out all around him, and he didn't even have to make up stories; the stories were around him too. We have to do it *all,* including the impossible or all but impossible task: make up a language as you go along. All you have to do to be a good novelist is to be like God on the first day.
—Walker Percy to Shelby Foote, October 19, 1973

There's no such thing as a sovereign and underived text.
—Walker Percy, "Herman Melville"

In *Fiction and Repetition,* J. Hillis Miller writes that his book concerns not so much "what" texts mean but "how" they mean. He explores narrative patterns, and what he finds is that narratives depend on repetition to generate meaning: "This book is an exploration of some of the ways [novels] work to generate meaning or to inhibit the too easy determination of a meaning based on the linear sequence of the story. . . . Any novel is a complex tissue of repetition and of repetitions within repetition, or of repetitions linked in chain fashion to other repetitions."[1] Miller's comment sounds similar to some advice Walker Percy got from Caroline Gordon when he was going through his years of novelistic apprenticeship. Percy sent his manuscripts of "The Charterhouse" and "The Gra-

1. J. Hillis Miller, *Fiction and Repetition* (Cambridge, Mass., 1982), 2–3.

mercy Winner" to Gordon, who obviously read his work very carefully; she responded to his first novel in about forty pages of singled-spaced prose. Many of those comments did not relate specifically to Percy's work, but dealt generally with novels, the task of the novelist, and writing. In short, she set forth her "theory" of the novel and applied it to Percy's work. One item she passed on seems especially pertinent to the question of repetition and writing. Gordon relates part of a conversation she had with a rural black preacher, who told her about his technique of delivering sermons: "First I tells'em I'm going to tell'em. Then I tell'em. Then I tell'em I done told'em."[2]

From one perspective the preacher's comment would seem to give moral latitude to the centuries-old problem of sleep and the sermon. It would also suggest a reason for the sometimes lifeless structure of some works of literary criticism, which often follow the introduction ("I tells'em I'm going to tell'em")-body ("I tell'em")-conclusion ("I tell'em I done told'em") format. Yet viewed differently the comment can quicken both homiletic and critical practice. For the preacher's words do what they say. The "what" and the "how" interpenetrate. The repetition of the verb "to tell," for example, is not a repetition without a difference. The threefold "tell'em" is compressed and encompassed by "tells'em" and "told'em," which mark the transition from the ideal or the possible to the actual. And "done told'em" repeats the auxiliary form of "going to tell'em," yet, while the auxiliaries are obviously different, the progression of sounds from "done" to "told" and the repetition of sounds in "going" and "told" ("gō" and "tō") signals on a smaller scale precisely what Miller writes about on a larger one. Furthermore, the self-enfolding and extended rhythms of the first and the last phrases find counterpoint in the pithy rhythm of the middle sentence, which nevertheless stresses the same verb. The middle sentence, in turn, is repeated in the first part of the third sentence. In his comment the preacher engages in what has often been considered the golden rule of all homiletics, and he thus displays his own moral integrity: he practices what he preaches! Gordon passes on the remark to Percy because, like J. Hillis Miller, she sees this repetition as efficacious in writing as well.

In order for repetition to work in writing, though, it has to be seen as

2. Caroline Gordon to Walker Percy, December 11, 1951, in Percy Papers, SHC.

more than a simple restating. It has to be a restating that incorporates identity and difference, limits and possibilities, the ideal and the actual. It has to be like the coach horn Constantin Constantius praises in Kierkegaard's *Repetition:* "Long live the stagecoach horn! It is the instrument for me for many reasons, and chiefly because one can never be certain of wheedling the same notes from this horn. A coach horn has infinite possibilities."[3] It is interesting to note that in his admiration of the coach horn, Constantin ostensibly wants to prove the impossibility of repetition. Yet here again Kierkegaard masters his irony. For the very difference in similarity (the instrument is the same instrument no matter how often one "wheedles" different notes from it) is precisely what repetition is all about. To approach repetition and *graphein* in the context of Percy's own narrative technique, then, I will inevitably have to repeat myself—with difference.

Chapter 1 deals with something of the "how" of repetition, autobiography, and Percy's works. Chapters 2 and 3 engage the "what." Yet in Percy the "how" and the "what" cannot be so easily separated. I agree with John W. Stevenson, who has argued that "the distinctive character of [Percy's] style is the particular way he uses language and the way this language controls and discovers its proper form. I suppose I am trying to say that Percy's art (his craft) is as much a part of his theme as is the theme itself."[4] Thus, I hope to show that repetition is not only a theme of Percy's work but that it informs his narrative style as well. I have already suggested such a notion when I argued that, like Kierkegaard, Percy uses the aesthetic to approach the religious. Another way of saying this is to say that *inter esse* finds embodiment in an "interesting" style. That style, furthermore, is fundamentally autobiographical.

In Chapter 1, I refer to James Olney's assertion that the essential autobiographical movement takes place in memory, in the interplay of past and present. In the context of their present consciousness, autobiographers grasp together into narrative form their past experience. But this "grasping together" (I borrow the concept from Paul Ricoeur) in memory and narrative is never a simple recapitulation of past events.[5] The story and the life

3. Kierkegaard, *Fear and Trembling/Repetition,* 175.

4. John W. Stevenson, "Walker Percy: The Novelist as Poet," *Southern Review,* n.s., XVII (1981), 165.

5. Paul Ricoeur, "Narrative Time," *Critical Inquiry,* VII (1980), 169–90.

are never identical. Rather, a distance, a gap, a difference always exists between the past as it was lived and the past as it is written. Yet as different as they are, lived life and written life, some connection must exist between them, else why bother to write in the first place? Thus, autobiography repeats the life of its subject (the self) in a way that joins identity and difference without a simple synthesis. Furthermore, as the terminal root of the word *autobiography, graphein* provides the link between the *autos* and *bios*. It enacts the repetition I have already addressed (the "what"), while it also engages in its own repetition (the "how"). Thus, some further thoughts on Percy's views of the self and life—and their relation to autobiography in general—will be necessary to examine repetition and writing. Most notably, I will return to some aspects of his language theory, especially with regard to metaphor and naming. In so doing, I too hope to link identity and difference. I hope to sound the coach horn. That is, I hope to practice what I preach.

Percy's fascination with language extends to every facet of his life and work, especially his analysis of "death-in-life." Although the resurgence of Gnostic thought has much to do with the "Century of Death" I outlined in the last chapter, the death of language, as Percy sees it, also contributes to the "peculiar malaise" he analyzes in his works. A central issue of all of his fiction, but more explicitly in *The Thanatos Syndrome,* concerns what Father Smith calls "the evacuation of signs." "[Words] don't signify anymore," he tells Tom More, and he goes on to make a direct link between the deprivation of signs and the murder of the Jews, for him the only sign that has not been evacuated (*TS,* 121). Father Smith implies that when signs have been deprived, so too has the sign user. Given such a state, any level of bestialism becomes possible.

If the entrance into sign use marks the passage into full humanity and thus elevates the sign user from an animal-like existence, as in the case of Helen Keller, then a loss of the signifying capacity of language divests humans of their unique humanity. For Percy, Keller's experience at the well house is paradigmatic. Everyone who is able to read these words has crossed the same threshold. I have already suggested that this primordial naming event is itself a repetition because it links concept and percept, the ideal and the actual. Somewhere along the way, however, words lose their signifying potential. They become evacuated. The signified and the signifier interpenetrate. It is important to note that this potential devolution rests in the same primordial naming act. Thus, naming possesses a dual nature. It has a capacity to reveal *and* conceal—or, as Charles Bigger writes, it is both a "call by Being and a violence against Being." That with which we know the world is also that which blocks that same knowing.[6]

In the Intermezzo of *Lost in the Cosmos,* to repeat more ground, Percy implies that art, as a naming event, also displays this same duality. On the one hand, it resists the interpenetration of the signifier by the signified; it frustrates the evacuation of signs. On the other hand, it is limited in this capacity because of its very use of signs. The epigraphs that head this chapter further indicate the dual nature of art as naming. According to the first, novelists, like God, create *ex nihilo.* When they name, they create in a sense an entirely new world. According to the second, novelists, like humans, are limited by texts that have gone before theirs. They rename or renovate what has been named but forgotten, or they name something that has been but has never been named before. The first reiterates Percy's call for the novelist to "sing a new song." The second indicates the limits of that very endeavor. Yet in its limitation, it also discloses possibility.

For Percy the social character of naming, the pairing of namer and hearer (or writer and reader), opens the possibility for a "co-celebration" of a thing beheld in common. The name sanctions and frees. The two impossibilities to which Percy refers in the epigraphs—the impossibility of creating a new language and the impossibility of creating a sovereign text—join possibility and limitation. They both invoke hope: the first, that something entirely new will be sung; the second, that at least something old will be sung in a new way. This linking of possibility and limitation forms, I think, the mystery of language and narrative, and it will guide my remarks in this chapter. For, Gabriel Marcel writes, "I cannot place myself outside or before [the encounter with mystery]; I am engaged in this encounter, I depend on it, I am inside it in a certain sense, it envelopes me and it compre-

6. Charles P. Bigger, "Walker Percy and the Resonance of the Word," *Southern Quarterly,* XVIII (1980), 47; see Lawson, "The Cross and the Delta," in *Walker Percy: Novelist and Philosopher,* ed. Gretlund and Westharp, 3–12.

hends me—even if it is not comprehended by me."[7] If I substitute the word *language* for *mystery* in Marcel's definition, the meaning remains unchanged. For language is precisely that which "envelopes and comprehends" the language user but that itself remains elusive. Perhaps nowhere can this mystery of language be better revealed (and concealed!) than in an exploration of metaphor and Percy's works, both fiction and nonfiction. For Percy understands metaphor, like the novel, as both inventive and derivative, something newly made, yet something made new, something renovated—something repeated.

In "Metaphor as Mistake" (1958), Percy explores the analogical and cognitive dimensions of metaphor, and he contends that in metaphor "something very big happens in a very small space" (*MB*, 66). That something very big is nothing less than the ontological potential of language and metaphor, their capacity to validate and discover being. For Percy claims ultimately that "metaphor is the true maker of language" (*MB*, 79). Returning once again to his favorite example, Helen Keller and the primordial naming act, Percy anticipates the writings of Paul Ricoeur on metaphor. Although Ricoeur notes that metaphor is a "phenomenon of predication, not denomination," on the level of the sentence and not of the single word, both writers agree that metaphor "tells us something new about reality." It is important to remember that, despite his repeated use of the Helen Keller phenomenon, Percy understands naming to extend beyond the level of isolated words. A symphony, a novel, a short story, a poem can all "name" and thus disclose being. They can, as Ricoeur puts it in *Time and Narrative,* "refigure" reality.[8] I will touch on this aspect of naming in the second section of this chapter. Suffice it to say now that although Percy uses "naming" to designate his understanding of metaphor, he uses it in a sense different from Ricoeur's "denomination."

For Percy the Helen Keller phenomenon offers fertile ground for an exploration of metaphor because in this "aboriginal naming act . . . the most obscure and the most creative of metaphors" manifests itself: "No

7. Gabriel Marcel, *The Philosophy of Existentialism* (New York, 1956), 22.
8. Paul Ricoeur, *Interpretation Theory: Discourse and the Surplus of Meaning* (Fort Worth, 1976), 50; Paul Ricoeur, *Time and Narrative* (3 vols.; Chicago, 1984, 1986, 1988). Here I refer to Ricoeur's tripartite development of "figuration, configuration, and refiguration."

modern poem was ever as obscure as Miss Sullivan's naming water *water* for Helen Keller." The word water has only the "most tenuous analogical similarities" with the thing itself (*MB,* 78, 79). The aboriginal naming act, which is metaphor, involves a pairing of word and thing, object beheld and word uttered. Percy writes: "We can only *conc*eive being, sidle up to it by laying something else alongside. We approach the thing not directly but by pairing, by apposing symbol and thing."[9] By virtue of the space between the word and the thing, language both validates and obscures; it responds to the call of being and does violence against it. When a namer utters a name in good faith and authority for a hearer, the thing beheld in common is both sanctioned and freed: sanctioned because the name somehow formulates, *i.e.,* gives form to, the being of what is commonly beheld; freed because that same formulation nevertheless makes a clearing for the thing to appear in all its strangeness. In its pairing, naming thus becomes a sort of "reconciliation," as Charles Bigger puts it.

Yet this same pairing leads to the deadening of language. Words no longer signify. Instead, the distance collapses, and words mummify what they originally disclosed. For the person who has long since crossed the linguistic threshold, the word *water* has devolved. Certainly I do not disclose being to you when I say *water* and point to the clear liquid that flows from a fountain. Signifier and signified have interpenetrated, and the word has lost its metaphorical potency. It has become evacuated. Ricoeur writes that "there are no live metaphors in the dictionary," and by this I take him to mean that if naming does not both validate and obscure, language is dead.[10]

It is the task of metaphor, then, to reinstate the distance between word and thing. Like naming, metaphor also employs a pairing, although it is often considered a "wrong" coupling. But in the "wrongness" of its pairing, its strange coupling, metaphor reopens the queerness and obscurity of being—its uncanniness. Ricoeur notes that metaphor's function is "close to what Gilbert Ryle has called a 'category mistake.' It is . . . a calculated error, which brings together things that do not go together and by means of this

9. *MB,* 72. "Symbol" here refers to "sign." In this essay Percy used the vocabulary of Cassirer and Langer instead of De Saussure.

10. Bigger, "Resonance of the Word," 47; Ricoeur, *Interpretation Theory,* 52.

apparent misundersanding [sic] it causes a new, hitherto unnoticed, relation of meaning to spring up between the terms that previous systems of classification had ignored or not allowed."[11] Thus, in "Metaphor as Mistake," Percy agrees with Gabriel Marcel who says that when "I ask what something is, I am more satisfied to be given a name even if the name means nothing to me (especially if?), than to be given a scientific classification" (*MB*, 72). Metaphor circumvents the abstract and general classifications that theory and science depend on, categories that make individual entities a "case of" or an "instance of" a general, discarnate rule. In this function of metaphor, the relation between Gnosticism, death-in-life, and language becomes most clear. For if language merely provides a means of conveying discarnate, theoretical categories, then it bypasses lived time in favor of an immediate perception of the atemporal abstract. Theory, then, becomes more real than the concrete, and a "loss of the creature" ensues.

Ricoeur argues that in its wrongness, metaphor not only circumvents previous systems of classification, but it depends on a "literal interpretation [an interpretation based on prevalent systems of classification] which self-destructs in a significant contradiction."[12] This notion of circumventing and destroying normal classification not only fits in with the "apocalyptic" theme of Percy's fiction (the de-struction of everyday contexts) and his avowed writing habits (an exercise in despair and recovery), but it also relates to a comment he once made to a French interviewer: "Recently I have read a book, you must read it: *Zen and the Art of Motorcycle Maintenance* by Robert Pirsig. I had been put off by the title a long time, but then I started reading it, and it certainly set me thinking. There are books, you know, even if you do not admire them, they give impetus to your mind. In that book the hero makes Aristotle and his logic responsible for all our evils—I personally make Descartes responsible—and has a nervous breakdown, which he overcomes by running and maintaining a motor-bike" (*Con*, 247). One wonders if it is both Aristotle's logic and his "classifications" that provided the "impetus" to Percy's mind in the reading of Pirsig's book. If it is both, then Ricoeur's comments about metaphor and classification would seem all the more apposite.

11. Bigger, "Resonance of the Word," *passim;* Ricoeur, *Interpretation Theory,* 52.
12. Ricoeur, *Interpretation Theory,* 50.

For Percy, Gerard Manley Hopkins creates metaphors that self-destruct best and so are thereby most able to capture the peculiar inscape of things. Lightning is not simply a flash of light in the sky but "a straight stroke, broad like a stroke with chalk and liquid, as if the blade of an oar just stripped open a ribbon seat in smooth water and it caught the light" (quoted in *MB*, 78). Hopkins was surely the kind of poet Percy had in mind when he wrote that a poet can "wrench [a] signifier out of context and exhibit it in all its queerness" (*LC*, 105).

But metaphor does not merely rename what has already been named and subsequently ossified, as in the case of "lightning." It also institutes something altogether new. It names what has been "secretly apprehended" (inscape) but hitherto unknown because unnamed. Metaphor, then, both renovates and invents. In either case it establishes in the reader or hearer "a unique joy which marks man's ordainment to being and the knowing of it" (*MB*, 71). It repeats the primordial naming act, and thus opens a new world and a new way of knowing the "old" world. It creates a new language.

Percy's thoughts on metaphor and language find a parallel in the writing of Paul John Eakin on autobiography. In a seminal chapter of his *Fictions in Autobiography: Studies in the Art of Self-Invention,* Eakin outlines "the relative positions of self and language in the order of being. . . . When an 'I' speaks, and especially in autobiographical discourse, is its language in effect an original speech, a self-validating testimony to the uniqueness of the self? Or is such speech always fatally derivative?" Eakin shows how questions of the relation between self and writing have polarized into "a self-before-language or a language-before-self set of positions."[13] Instead of adopting one pole or the other, Eakin looks for a third way, a position I characterize as "self-in-language."

Borrowing insights from a wide spectrum of linguistic philosophers, developmental psychologists, literary theorists, and autobiographers—some of whom were Percy's own favorites, notably Susanne Langer and Helen Keller—Eakin argues that "the origin of the self as the reflexive center of human subjectivity is inextricably bound up with the activity of language." He posits a model, based on three moments, for "the history of self-defini-

---

13. Paul John Eakin, the chapter "Self-Invention in Autobiography: The Moment of Language," in *Fictions in Autobiography*, 181–82, 191.

tion" of an individual. The first moment involves the acquisition of language, whereby the self becomes aware of itself; the second concerns what some have termed the "I-am-me" experience, in which the self undergoes a doubling of self-consciousness, *i.e.,* a "self-conscious experience of self-consciousness"; and the third, if it ever comes, is the autobiographical act, which "like the first moment . . . is a coming together of self and language; [and] like the second . . . is characterized by a double reflexiveness. . . . The text of an autobiography is likely to recapitulate the second moment as a content, while the making of the text re-enacts the first moment as a structure."[14]

Put in terms I developed earlier in this chapter, Eakin seems to say that the act of autobiography repeats both the acquisition of language (as the "how" of the text) and the experience of self as self (as the "what" of the text). Autobiography creates a new language that both comprehends and constitutes the self even as its content is derived from a self already experienced as a self determined and immeshed in language. Thus, autobiography evinces what J. Hillis Miller says about novels being "a complex tissue of repetition and of repetitions within repetition." In Percy's terms, autobiography evinces the "consciousness raised to the second power," which he understands true Kierkegaardian repetition to be (*MB*, 96). Autobiography attempts to name the self—*i.e.,* to sanction and free it—in the self-consciousness of language. It repeats the aboriginal naming act, and thus it provides, as Olney's classic work suggests, a "metaphor of self."

It may be useful to examine Eakin's analysis of Helen Keller's experience at the well house to show further the convergence (and divergence) of his and Percy's thought and to show what I see as Percy's contribution to the understanding of autobiography as metaphorical repetition.[15] Eakin reveals how Helen Keller's experience is similar to the autobiographical act in three respects: "it is an act of memory ('suddenly I felt . . . a thrill of returning thought'); it is an act of language in which experience is transformed into symbol ('she spelled into the other [hand] the word *water*. . . . my whole attention fixed upon the motion of her fingers'); and it is a consti-

---

14. *Ibid.*, 198–219.

15. It may also be useful for readers to look again at Keller's description of this moment. I have quoted the entire passage in note 9 of Chapter 2.

tution of self ('that living word awakened my soul')." Eakin goes on to say that her experience taught her that "the self has a name," and that it is the task of autobiography "to state 'what we have learned we are.'"[16] In this sense, then, autobiography would be both invention and derivation: invention because it constitutes the self; derivation because it depends on the what the self "has learned" but hitherto left unnamed. Is it possible to say that autobiography, like Percy's metaphor, tries to capture the "inscape" of the self's experience of self, to capture the secretly apprehended but hitherto unnamed selfhood of the self, its "unformulated presence?" (*MB* 69). If so, this task, according to Percy, both discloses and does violence to whatever being the self may have.

Eakin often worries about, but cannot resolve, the challenge Jacques Derrida poses to the relation of self and language. For Derrida and his followers, writing can never manifest the self-presence, "the meeting point of the physical and the intelligible," that we accept as the norm in speech.[17] Thus, autobiography can never make present a self that is never self-present. Like Eakin, I cannot claim to resolve the metaphysical question of self and language, but I can repeat some aspects of Percy's thought on the question in an effort toward that end. In Chapter 2 I made much of "the unformulability of the self," that the self, as Percy claims, names everything under the sun except itself. The self has no sign of itself. In the case of Binx Bolling, I argued that although the self cannot find a single sign for itself, its only avenue toward self-discovery nevertheless rests in sign use, that is, language. Thus, as a pairing of word and thing, the aboriginal naming act is bound to be frustrated when it turns toward the self, because the self is "nothing." No single word can encompass it. On the other hand, metaphor, as a pairing of one named thing with another ("flesh is grass")—an activity, as I have tried to show, that repeats both the aboriginal naming act and the acquisition of language—*can* provide an avenue to the self. In its queer, "wrong" pairing, metaphor can repeat the queerness of the self that has "fallen" into language. The self is a stranger and, with the help of meta-

16. Eakin, *Fictions in Autobiography*, 212–13.

17. Jonathan Culler, "Jacques Derrida," in *Structuralism and Since: From Lévi-Strauss to Derrida*, ed. John Sturrock (New York, 1981), 169–70 (quoted in Eakin, *Fictions in Autobiography*, 224).

phor's indirection, it can constitute and disclose its own strangeness. One is reminded of the subtitle of Percy's *The Message in the Bottle: How Queer Man Is, How Queer Language Is, and What One Has to Do with the Other*. In this sense Binx Bolling's experience of people as "dead dead dead" can be likened to dead metaphor. According to Binx, too many people "go gently into" a good dictionary. They accept some theoretical formulation of the self based on the tenets and classifications of scientific humanism, which would deny their queerness. They accept themselves as cases or instances of this or that abstraction.

This notion of strangeness, furthermore, provides an avenue for extending Eakin's lucid analysis of Helen Keller's experience. To the threefold similarity he cites between her experience and autobiography, I would add Keller's last sentence: "It would have been difficult to find a happier child than I was as I lay in my crib at the close of that eventful day and lived over the joys it had brought me, and for the first time longed for a new day to come." Here, Keller repeats ("live[s] over") the events of the day, not only in her crib, but also in the act of writing her text and in the text itself. The repetition adds a new dimension to her existence: for the first time in her life she has a future. She "long[s] for a new day to come." She longs, in essence, for the opportunity to repeat events, new and old; that is, she has entered into "anticipatory resoluteness." Like Melville, Keller "marks [her] birth" from that day. But the longing, like the "repentance and sorrow" she experienced at the breaking of her doll, indicates the very queerness, the strangeness of her newfound existence as a human. One neither longs nor feels strange if one is "at home." Only *homo viator* longs. Keller's entry into language, then, also marks her entry into the restlessness of her own unformulability, an *inter esse* that is a happiness, to be sure, but a happy longing. Her entry into language and the language she employs to tell of that event (the text) are self-reflexive. I mean to say that her entry into language becomes the metaphor for herself, a story in which the "how" and the "what" interpenetrate to disclose a self now happy and strange but never quite itself.[18]

One of the places the "how" and the "what" overlap for Percy comes

18. See also Percy's comments in the foreword to Henry Kisor's *What's That Pig Outdoors? A Memoir of Deafness* (New York, 1990), especially viii.

in the account of the "blue-dollar hawk." He first uses the story in "Metaphor as Mistake" as one of the opening examples of the sort of "misnaming" that can result in an "authentic poetic experience" (*MB*, 65). Portions of the story reappear years later as part of the older Will Barrett's "memory trip" in *The Second Coming*. As in any true repetition, the two versions display both similarities and differences. Undoubtedly, some of the differences result from the demands of the particular rhetorical situations. An essay on the ontology of metaphor requires a clearer demonstration of a thesis than does a section of a novel. Yet the very differences are themselves posited on a prior acknowledgment of similarity. Thus, the way Percy employs the story in the novel suggests that he repeats his previous work to reveal something about Barrett, something about the novel as a whole, and something about his narrative technique in general.

In "Metaphor as Mistake," the account goes as follows:

> I remember hunting as a boy in south Alabama with my father and brother and a Negro guide. At the edge of some woods we saw a wonderful bird. He flew as swift and straight as an arrow, then all of a sudden folded his wings and dropped like a stone into the woods. I asked what the bird was. The guide said it was a blue-dollar hawk. Later my father told me the Negroes had got it wrong: It was really a blue darter hawk. I can still remember my disappointment at the correction. What was so impressive about the bird was its dazzling speed and the effect of alternation of its wings, as if it were flying by a kind of oaring motion. (*MB*, 64)

I want to examine two aspects of this personal account. First, it rings true. As Percy writes, "everyone has a blue-dollar hawk in his childhood" (*MB*, 69). One of my own, for example, must have been rather common for a child growing up at the time because I have heard others recount something similar. Louisiana had renewed its interest in its French roots through various grammar-school programs. Yet being part of a middle-class, suburban (*i.e.,* ahistorical) family, I really had little idea of what "French roots" meant. Thus, when I heard my parents and siblings speak of job possibilities and perquisites that certain companies provided for their employees and/or customers, I mistook "fringe benefits" for "French benefits." For the longest time I tried to understand just what sort of benefits were being provided. When I learned the correct form, I shrugged at my own denseness, and I felt a bit chastened and disappointed that the "real" term was so straightforward. But I haven't forgotten the attempt to connect what little I knew of the business world with what little I knew of the French. "French benefits" said much more than its descriptive counterpart. But then I was only a boy.

When he first saw the hawk, Percy was a boy, too. This is the second aspect of the account I want to examine: while Percy is free with the first-person pronoun in the account of the hunting trip with his father, the person to whom he refers when he cites the example in the rest of the essay is not the "I" of the present writer, now reflecting on the ontology of metaphor by means of an experience he had as a child, but "the boy" who had the experience (see especially *MB,* 71). Like Henry Adams, Percy eschews the use of the first-person pronoun for the third person. I do not want to make too much of this shift in shifters. Certainly it is due in part to the fact that the example supports the thesis Percy pursues in the piece. In such a "scientific" essay he removes himself from the writing so that the general idea may be more easily apprehended by the reader. Yet could one not say that in his retrieval of the memory Percy also retrieves and then distances himself from the disappointment he originally experienced at his father's correction? Furthermore, could we not say that, even here, Percy rejects his father's foreclosing of the possibility of being? [19]

In the account as he writes it, it is "I" who "can still remember the disappointment." Yet everywhere else in the piece it is "the boy's delight," "the boy can't help but be disappointed," "the boy's preference," and so on (*MB,* 71). Thus, the philosopher of language now sitting at his desk in Covington, Louisiana, seems to forget the "I" of his account and to posit someone quite other ("the boy") who experienced the wonder and disappointment of the name and its subsequent correction. This strange shift between "I" and "the boy" opens a distance that can be viewed as a repetition of the strange distance in metaphor that, of course, forms part of the content, the "what," of the essay. However obscure and distanced, then, the essay is not only about the mistake upon which metaphor inevitably depends, it also enacts that same mistake by distancing the writer from "the boy," and then both from the father, who proved so disappointing. In the language of the

19. I am following William Rodney Allen's reading of Percy's work, though not his non-fiction, in light of the "father." See Allen, *A Southern Wayfarer.*

text Percy repeats the argument of the text itself: language and metaphor mediate experience by means of distance and indirection. The writer can never relive the experience as it was lived by the boy; he can only write it. In the writing Percy seems to evince something of Keller's discovery of longing, for he, too, seems to long for a time before his disappointment. Like Keller, he senses an unformulability that nevertheless calls for formulation in language. The writing, however wrong, remains the only avenue through which the experience might be both renovated and created. It provides Percy with a link between his *autos* and *bios*. "Metaphor as Mistake" thus becomes part of the mistaken metaphor by which the "I" of the writer reconciles himself with "the boy" of the experience. In this essay Percy not only adds to his reader's understanding of the relation between metaphor and the queerness of language and being, but he reveals his own concealment in metaphor (his own strangeness) as well. He discloses himself as "enveloped" and "comprehended" in the mystery of language.

If it is true that Percy turned from writing essays to writing novels because he wanted to emulate the French, who "see nothing wrong with writing novels that address what they consider the deepest philosophical issues" (*Con,* 183), then his use of the blue-dollar hawk account in *The Second Coming* would seem to confirm his self-stated purpose. Whereas the account in "Metaphor as Mistake" serves as an example that supports a philosophical thesis, in the novel it becomes an episode that finds its place in a larger configuration. But in the type of novels that Percy writes, the account should nevertheless serve something of its original philosophical purpose. I want to explore Percy's fictional repetition of this account to see what light it can shed on his "repetitive" narrative technique as a whole, especially with regard to plot and metaphor.

In some of his early essays and interviews Percy often made comments that suggest a lack of concern with plots: "I'm not primarily concerned with plotting a story"; "by following a predestined plan with outline, like some writers, I could foresee the action and likely it wouldn't go veering off on another path. But I can't work like that" (*Con,* 24, 8). To Shelby Foote, who often tried to goad Percy into working from an outline—Foote himself seemed obsessed with plotting—Percy once wrote: "The French really kill me—it's *all* form. Come to think of it, you would like them better than I do." And later he wrote: "The French are idealogues, *i.e.,* madmen, and yet without them we'd sink into a torpor. The mind-body split, locked-in ghost in a machine on one side, structure and world on the other, me with the former, you with the latter, like I used to make ghostly spiritual (but flyable) Lockheed Vegas and you used to make solid structural admirable perfect unflyable P-51s."[20] And toward the end of "From Facts to Fiction" (1966), a piece about "how it came to pass that a physician turned writer and became a novelist," Percy refers to John Barth's comment that the age of the nineteenth-century novel has passed: "I agree. When I sat down to write *The Moviegoer,* I was very much aware of discarding the conventional notions of a plot and a set of characters, discarded because the traditional concept of plot-and-character reflects a view of reality which has been called into question."[21]

Despite these disavowals of structure and plot (and what seems to be a backhanded swipe at Foote's work), Percy, like any writer, nevertheless *has* to plot his novels. His stories have to be "followable."[22] Since the "traditional concept of plot-and-character reflects a view of reality that has been called into question," it seems likely that Percy turned once again to his philosophical mentor, who called much into question, to derive and create his narrative technique. In *Repetition,* Constantin suggests that *"repetition* is a crucial expression for what 'recollection' was to the Greeks. Just as they taught that all knowing is a recollecting, modern philosophy will teach that all life is a repetition."[23] If Kierkegaard is right, then it would seem likely that narrative, the primary means by which we know life, would also evince repetition. I have already cited J. Hillis Miller's and Caroline Gordon's references to narrative repetition. In "Narrative Time," Paul Ricoeur has also written on the subject, and his thought helps to clarify the type of plotting that Percy turns to in the wake of the collapse of the "traditional" novel.

In this essay that seems to serve as a short recapitulation of his three-

20. Walker Percy to Shelby Foote, November 28, 1977, March 4, 1978, both in Percy Papers, SHC.
21. *Signposts,* 186, 190. In another interview Percy seems to contradict what he says about Barth's view; see *Con,* 24–25.
22. See Ricoeur, "Narrative Time," 174ff.
23. Kierkegaard, *Fear and Trembling/Repetition,* 131.

volume opus, *Time and Narrative,* Ricoeur suggests that "every narrative combines two dimensions in various proportions, one chronological and the other nonchronological. The first may be called the episodic dimension, which characterizes the story as made out of events. The second is the configurational dimension, according to which the plot construes significant wholes out of scattered events. . . . I understand [the configurational act] to be the act of the plot, as eliciting a pattern from a succession." Despite their relationship of polarity with respect to chronology, both episode and configuration evince temporality. The episodic dimension "tends toward the linear representation of time." The succession and progression of episodes reflects the "irreversible order of time common to human and physical events." The configurational dimension, however, "is more deeply temporal than the time of merely episodic narratives." Ricoeur suggests that configuration imposes Kermode's "sense of an ending." When a story becomes well known "retelling takes the place of telling. . . . Then following the story is less important than apprehending the well-known end as implied in the beginning and the well-known episodes as leading to this end." Time is not nullified "by the teleological structure of the judgment which grasps together the events under the heading of 'the end.'" Rather, this grasping together in configuration involves a deepening of time; it involves repetition: "By reading the end in the beginning and the beginning in the end, we learn also to read time itself backward. . . . In this way, a plot establishes human action not only within time . . . but within memory." Furthermore, memory is not on the level of episodic time. Rather, "it is the spiral movement that, through anecdotes and episodes, brings us back to the almost motionless constellation of potentialities that the narrative retrieves. The end of the story is what equates the present with the past, the actual with the potential. The hero *is* who he *was.*" This narrative repetition possesses a forward movement as well; it discloses "the complete retrieval in resoluteness of . . . inherited potentialities." Spanos' view of repetition as both a mnemonic and projective activity converges with Ricoeur's. I'm not sure, however, that Spanos would appreciate the company.[24]

24. Ricoeur, "Narrative Time," 178–80, 186. For a similar view, see Stephen Crites, "The Narrative Quality of Experience," *Journal of the American Academy of Religion,* XXXIV (1971), 291–311, rpr. in *Why Narrative? Readings in Narrative Theology,* ed. Stanley Hauerwas and L. Gregory Jones (Grand Rapids, Mich., 1989), 65–88.

It seems to me that all of Percy's novels display the type of narrative repetition of which Ricoeur writes. *The Moviegoer,* for example, begins with a "spiraling" and layering of memory. The first three paragraphs take the reader from the present of Binx's receiving a note from his aunt to the memory of his brother's death to the memory of going to a movie with Linda. Then Binx gives a description of his life in Gentilly. We are not brought back to the present until page eleven. In those same pages Binx introduces us to ideas of certification, the search, science, consumerism, and stoicism, all of which will find further elaboration and repetition as the novel progresses.

Furthermore, the beginning and end both concern death, as does a good deal of the middle, although death of a different sort. Scott's death is recounted in the beginning as a memory, and the epilogue recounts the story of Binx's and Kate's visit with Lonnie the day before his death. This account is also out of sequence with the present of the epilogue. After Scott dies, Aunt Emily enjoins Binx to "act like a soldier," thus inviting him to become a "southern stoic."[25] But Binx embraces a Christian view of death when Lonnie dies. One of Lonnie's brothers asks Binx: "When Our Lord raises us up on the last day, will Lonnie still be in a wheelchair or will he be like us?" "He'll be like you," Binx responds (*MG,* 240). Thus while the two accounts repeat one another and provide a frame for the action of the novel, they do not establish a relationship of circularity and closure. Rather, their relation manifests the "retrieval of inherited potentialities" from the narrative. Binx tells us at one point that he is at home neither in his aunt's stoicism nor his mother's Catholicism. At the end, however, he recapitulates (and capitulates to) both of these "potentialities"—he goes to medical school as his aunt had wished, and he affirms a Christian view of death, and life. Thus, he is who he was, both the same and other. The end repeats the beginning, and to read this novel from the end foregrounds Binx's wanderings throughout the book. Just as Binx retrieves the "inherited potentialities" from the two sides of his family, the narrative retrieves its own possibilities into a configuration of pilgrimage.

Thus, the narrative repetition in *The Moviegoer* takes place on an even

---

25. *MG,* 4. Lawson, "Walker Percy's Southern Stoic," in *Following Percy,* 41–63.

larger scale. In "Physician as Novelist" (1989), which is itself a repetition of "From Facts to Fiction," Percy reflects on his first novel:

> The novel, almost by accident, became a narrative of the search, the quest. And so the novel, again almost by accident—or was it accident?—landed squarely in the oldest tradition of Western letters: the pilgrim's search outside himself, rather than the guru's search within. All this happened to the novelist and his character without the slightest consciousness of a debt to St. Augustine or Dante. Indeed, the character creates within himself and within the confines of a single weekend in New Orleans a microcosm of the spiritual history of the West, from the Roman patrician reading his Greek philosophers to the thirteenth-century pilgrim who leaves home and takes to the road. (*Signposts*, 193)

The narrative inherits potentialities, then, not only from its own progression, but from the tradition of Western letters as a whole. *The Moviegoer* retrieves those possibilities and, like metaphor that both retrieves and creates, that posits something derivative and original, the novel renders them anew so that reader and writer (hearer and namer) may come together in a new/old metaphor for themselves. In its own derivation and originality, *The Moviegoer* sings a new song about something very old—the status of humans as neither angels nor beasts, neither theorists nor consumers, but as wayfaring pilgrims. Percy suggests, then, that because it calls for the destruction of foreclosed possibilities, the postmodern condition enables the retrieval of the "inherited potentiality" of pilgrimage.

The same sort of narrative repetition takes place in *The Second Coming*, especially in Chapter III, where the story of the blue-dollar hawk recurs. The very recurrence suggests the sort of retrieval Ricoeur writes of. Yet, as I hope to show, the retrieval of this particular episode in the larger configuration of this particular novel proves especially fruitful.

The Second Coming, like *The Thanatos Syndrome*, is something of a paradox in the Percy corpus. For one thing, it seems that Percy never anticipated writing another story about Will Barrett. On February 8, 1977, he wrote to Foote: "The only thing I'm sure of is that I can't do what you suggested, write a novel-type novel, the doings of Will Barrett after he leaves Santa Fe."[26] And to several interviewers after the book's publication,

26. Walker Percy to Shelby Foote, February 8, 1977, in Percy Papers, SHC.

Percy admitted that he was not aware that he was retelling the story of Will Barrett until he was a hundred or so pages into the novel (see *Con,* 183, 188, 194, 229). Yet this work, it seems, more than any other, not only returns to the earlier protagonist, but also presents itself as a "novel-type" novel. What I mean to say is that, while the work does not manifest an abandonment of his earlier view about the world of the traditional novel having passed away, it is nevertheless his most obviously structured and plotted work. The alternation of points of view from Will to Allie in the chapters of the first part and their coming together in Part Two manifest an unusual degree of structure for Percy. Furthermore, the "crisscross" pattern of the book—Will's "used up language" and Allie's fresh language, Will's memory and Allie's amnesia, Will's "sickness in health" and Allie's "health in sickness"—likewise points to Percy's concern with plot in this work. Moreover, the crisscross structure itself demands a retrieval of the "plot" at the beginning of each new chapter, at least in Part One, since it alternates between the points of view of the two main characters.

After the book's publication Percy was fond of telling interviewers that *The Second Coming* was "the first unalienated novel since Tolstoy" (see *Con,* 190, 235), and this would seem to place it in the tradition of the "classical" novel. In a way, then, the book's structure suggests the retrieval of the inherited potentialities of the traditional "novel-type" novel even as it works against such a generic conception of the novel. One would be hard pressed to find characters such as Will and Allie in any traditional novel unless one bypasses Tolstoy to enter the world of Walter and Tristram Shandy. Nevertheless, the book does present a "sense of an ending" and resolution very much different from Percy's previous works.

Now if one reads *The Second Coming* backwards, as Ricoeur suggests, from the perspective of its ending, then one could return to almost any chapter to find the end repeated and embedded in the beginning. Yet Chapter III, it seems to me, repeats more of Percy's philosophical concerns and points both backward and forward in the novel to the themes and imagery that are themselves repeated. In Chapter III, Miller's "complex tissue" of "repetition and repetitions within repetition" begins to manifest itself. The opening words of the chapter, for example—"undoubtedly something was happening to him"—repeat the vague "something" that haunts the opening lines of the novel: "The first sign that something had gone wrong manifested itself while he was playing golf. Or rather it was the first time he admitted to himself that something might be wrong" (*SC,* 44, 3). As the first chapter and the novel as a whole progress, the unusual "something," instead of gaining a simple clarification, becomes both clearer and more obscure. The definitions that presumably delimit this "something" offer only further possibilities. Is the something related to Will's chemistry or is it part of the "farcical" lives he and his fellows seem to be living? Is it depression or is it a normal response to a deranged world? The narrative raises but never responds directly to these questions.

The imagery of spraying or dispersion works in a similar fashion. The sand trap into which Will falls on the opening page is repeated in the "spraying sand" of Ed Cupp's "skulled" sand shot in Chapter III (68). Both, however, are recapitulated in the locker-room bar, which is "dominated by a photomural of Jack Nicklaus blasting out of a sand trap" (12). The photomural, in turn, is repeated enough—significantly in the penultimate sentence of Chapter III—to suggest its relation to Will's memory of his father's suicide. At the end of Chapter III the narrator tells us that Will's "entire life lay before him, beginning, middle, and end, as plain as the mural of Jack Nicklaus blasting out of the sand trap" (79). But this information comes only after Will has begun to reconstruct (as one does when one views a mural) the hunting trip in Thomasville with his father, the "most important event of his life" (3). Just as the locker-room bar is dominated by the mural of Nicklaus, Will's life is dominated by the memory of this hunting trip and his father's death.

In the account of the hunting trip the imagery of spraying recurs in the description of the father's gunshot that was meant to kill the boy: "The boy saw the muzzle burst and flame spurting from the gun like a picture of a Civil War soldier shooting" (56). Later, as his father denies the true intent of his shot, he tells his son through D'Lo (the maid): "I had no idea that savage [the shotgun] had a pattern that wide" (59). The "pattern" not only suggests the pattern of the book, but also patterns Will's description of the suicide. It has, in a sense, become so wide as to pattern Will's cosmos: "brain cells which together faltered and fell short, now flowered and flew apart, flung like stars around the whole dark world" (149).

It is while Will lay in the sand trap, too, that "a strange bird flew past" (3). The bird is not mentioned again until page 47, but there it is described in terms very similar to those in "Metaphor as Mistake": "Earlier he had seen a bird, undoubtedly some kind of a hawk, fly across the fairway straight as an arrow and with astonishing swiftness, across a ridge covered by scarlet and gold trees, then fold its wings and drop like a stone into the woods. It reminded him of something but before he could think what it was, sparks flew forward at the corner of his eye. He decided with interest that something was happening to him, perhaps a breakdown, perhaps a stroke" (47). Here, "straight as an arrow," "swift," and "drop like a stone into the woods" all repeat the depiction of the hawk in Percy's essay. But the description in the novel joins the elusive "something" with which the book and the chapter begin, a "something," moreover, that not only disperses Will's thought, but also is itself announced by "sparks," yet another image of spraying. Repetition discloses repetitions within repetition.

It is interesting to note, too, that the similes Percy employs to describe the hawk's flight in both the essay and the novel are clichés. They are the sorts of comparisons that no longer reveal but rather entomb. They are, in a sense, dead metaphors. A case could be made for Percy's use of such dried-up language in the essay. The main point of the blue-dollar hawk account is, after all, to show that the sort of misnaming that happened to the young Percy is itself metaphor. Thus, the similes used in describing the bird's flight are subservient, if you will, to the main type of misnaming that "blue-dollar hawk" manifests. An attempt to depict the bird's flight through vivid metaphor might have detracted from the point of the essay. Can the same be said for the account in the novel?

The second mention of the hawk occurs just after Will sinks an eagle putt. Despite the "something" that is happening to him, Will still muses on and enacts the "small rites" of golf: "He was of two minds, playing golf and at the same time wondering with no more than a moderate curiosity what was happening to him" (48). The hawk, however,

was not of two minds. Single-mindedly it darted through the mountain air and dove into the woods. Its change of direction from level flight to drop was fabled. That is, it made him think of times when people told him fabulous things and he believed them. Perhaps a Negro had told him once that this kind of hawk is the only bird in the world that can—can what? He remembered. He remembered everything today. The hawk, the Negro said, could fly full speed and straight into the hole of a hollow tree and brake to a stop inside. He, the

Negro, had seen one do it. It was possible to believe that the hawk could do just such a single-minded thing. (48)

The single-mindedness of the hawk retrieves elements of the account of the cat in Chapter I. The cat is "a hundred percent cat, no more no less"—*i.e.,* of one mind—but people are often only "two percent themselves"—*i.e.,* dispersed (16). And Will's double-mindedness repeats the effect of the play on personal pronouns in Allie's "Instructions from Myself to Myself" (27), in which she writes these sorts of sentences: "It took me (you? us?) all my life to make the discovery. Why so long? And then I (you, we) had to go crazy to do it" (40). Will's being of two minds also sets the stage for his meeting with Allie, his double, which takes place toward the end of the third chapter.

But the single-minded hawk and the double-minded Will also retrieve a major aspect of Percy's thought on language. Because of language, Percy argues, we experience a "semiotic fall," a consciousness of ourselves as knowers who can name and know everything in the world through the mediation of signs, everything, that is, except ourselves. With no name for the self, we are semiotically adrift, never quite ourselves. Since cats and hawks do not have language, they have not experienced the "fall" and thus are always 100 percent themselves. That the single-minded hawk is also "fabled" furthers the complexity of the novel's tissue.

From the Latin *fabula,* "a narrative, story," and *fari,* "to speak," "fabled" implies the hawk's "storied" or "spoken" existence. Although labeled "wonderful" in Percy's essay, the hawk is nowhere called "fabled." It becomes so only in the story about Will Barrett and in the story he reconstructs in his memory. Barrett's memory, in fact, can be seen as both the subject and the agent of much of *The Second Coming.* Like St. Augustine, who, as Stephen Crites points out, tries to "collect" his "dispersed" memories into a coherent form, Barrett struggles against the dispersion of himself as a son of his "dispersed" father.[27] He tries to "grasp together" a story that will "make sense" of both himself and his father. At one time, "fabled" suggests, this task was not so difficult. Barrett lived in a storied world: "when people told him fabulous things . . . he believed them." Now, however, the

---

27. Crites, "Narrative Quality," in *Why Narrative?,* ed. Hauerwas and Jones, 74.

only stories he hears are jokes, and what he hears is "not the joke, but the plan and progress of the joke," its structure (65).

It is noteworthy that Jimmy Rogers, the joke-teller in this scene, is described as being "all plans and schemes and deals" (59). The idea of plans is repeated in Chapter IV, when the narrator recounts Allie's struggles against the "plans" of her mother, her father, and Dr. Duk (89–94). She decides to make her own plans: "What if *I* make plans for me" (96). This resolve to act on her own carries over into her renovation of the greenhouse and stove. The idea of plans, furthermore, finds a place in the later chapters of the book when Leslie makes plans for Will and Will and Allie make plans for themselves.

The important point, however, is that Barrett's fabulous world has been shattered and, fittingly enough, it was shattered during his father's attempt to repeat a "fabled" hunt (53). But the fabled hawk and the fabled hunt do not imply the same thing. For the boy "fabled" suggests a vivid metaphor, a time when language was not dead, when stories quickened the sense of the world. It repeats, in short, the repetition that is enacted in the aboriginal naming act. That is to say, it discloses the possibility of being. But in the "fabled" of the father's hunt, one senses the entombment of language. Like Constantin Constantius' failed attempt to repeat his trip to Berlin in *Repetition,* the father cannot repeat the legendary hunting trip: "This hunt had gone badly. The Negro guide was no good. The dog had been trained badly. The lawsuit was not going well. They, the man and the boy, had spent a bad sleepless night in an old hotel (the same hotel where the man had spent the night before the great Thomasville hunt). The hotel was not at all as the man had remembered it" (53). Here "fabled" suggests the devolution of language, its capacity to do violence to being. Instead of opening possibilities, "fabled" in the father's case shuts off possibility, expressed quite literally in the father's attempt to kill both his son and himself. Unable to reckon with—unable to "story"—change in time, the father dispenses with language and memory in his cataclysmic self-dispersion. The "how" and the "what" intermesh. The novel both retrieves its own "inherited potentialities" and becomes the story of Barrett's struggle against his heritage. One could even say that the rest of the book concerns Barrett's search for a type of dispersion that paradoxically unifies. The sexual nature of the father's suicide—"the penetration and union of perfect cold gunmetal

into warm quailing mortal flesh, the coming to end all coming" (149) —
finds counterexpression in the "comings" (sexual and otherwise) that bring
Allie and Will together in their difference.

It is interesting to note that at the time of the hawk's third mention in
the chapter, Barrett's attitude toward the vague "something" that opens the
novel has shifted. At first the "something" seemed so dominant that "it
occurred to him that he might shoot himself" (4). Yet, as I have already
cited, when the hawk is mentioned a second time, the "something" holds
only "a moderate curiosity" (48). By the time the narrative returns to the
hawk, there is only a "mild stirring of curiosity. . . . A little something or
other was happening, but no more than that" (70). This shift seems to indicate Barrett's preliminary movement outside himself and the first hint of
his future possibility, for immediately following the description of the dim-
inution of the "something" we are told that "one day he heard a footstep.
Someone was coming" (70). At this point, of course, the "someone" is ambivalent. It could be the specter of his father, who lures Barrett toward self-
annihilation and *thanatos*. Or it could be the call of *eros:* in the very next
section of the chapter, as he hunts for his errant golf balls in the woods,
Will meets Allie for the first time.

The third mention of the hawk occurs just before their coming together. At the same time he heard the footstep, he "saw the bird. A small
cloud passed over the sun, the darkness settling so quickly it left the greens
glowing. A hawk flew over, a dagger-winged falcon, its flight swift and
single-minded and straight over the easy ambling golfers. When it reached
the woods it folded its wings as abruptly as if it had been shot and fell like
a stone."[28] The "cloud" retrieves the one he noticed as he lay in the sand
bunker on the novel's first page. There it is one that "went towering
thousands of feet into the air" and that looked like the cloud "over Hiro-
shima" (3). Just as the nondescript "something" has diminished, so have the
proportions of the cloud. The rest of the hawk's description is by now familiar: swift, straight, single-minded, fell like a stone. The distinguishing

---

28. *SC,* 70. Some parallels between the account of the hawk and that of the peregrine
falcon in *The Last Gentleman* suggest an even more complex tissue of repetition—*i.e.,* woods/
park, gun/telescope, "something"/"sign."

feature of this reference rests in the fact that the hawk is given a name. It is a dagger-winged falcon.

Artistic license surely allows Percy to change the names that appear in "Metaphor as Mistake"—"blue-dollar hawk" and "blue darter hawk." But the character of the name here seems more akin to the disappointing "description" the father gives the boy than it does to the more vivid and truer name the guide gives. "Dagger-winged," like "blue darter," suggests a class of bird, not its "inscape." If Will is awakening to the possibility of a future, if "someone is coming," and if the hawk is "fabled," then why would it be given a descriptive designation and not a name?

The important thing to remember here, it seems to me, is that Will is on a precipice. As the ambivalent use of "fabled" suggests, he is both on the verge of a reawakening and caught up in the death-dealings of his father. Since I am reading the book backwards, however, since I am retrieving the inherited potentialities from the end, then what seems to be a description can be seen instead as a reawakening into language. Like Paul John Eakin's tripartite analysis of Helen Keller's entry into language, "dagger-winged" signifies Will's nascent autobiographical act. First, it is an act of memory. Will remembers everything, the narrator says, and the name itself is part of this remembering. From this perspective "dagger-winged" becomes a name on a par with "water." Second, it is an act of language; experience is transformed into symbol. The hawk, before unnamed, is somehow formulated and set free under the auspices of "dagger-winged." Third, it is a constitution of self. Will's naming and renaming brings about "the second coming" of self with Allie. And finally, if I add the dimension of the future to Eakin's triad, the resolve to name further comes about by the grace of the "someone coming" to him. In the retrieval of this name from his memory, Will manifests the resolve to go on naming. This he does, not only in naming the before unnameable, as in the many "names of death" (246–48), but in his continued renaming, his reconstructing the "fable" of the hunting trip with his father. Having passed through the death of his father, Will now experiences the gain of repetition. "Dagger-winged falcon," then, like *The Second Coming,* is both something new and something derived. The hawk repeats the story as told in Percy's essay, but it introduces a new name. And the novel repeats itself so that it might grasp together the dispersed selves of Will and Allie—and the reader—into a new fable.

Percy was once asked in an interview if he was worried about repeating himself in *The Second Coming*. He responded: "It's been said that all novelists write the same novel over and over again. And since the kind of fiction I write is an exploration to begin with, all I can hope to do is push the boundaries back. I'm convinced that in *The Second Coming* there's a definite advance" (*Con*, 183–84). Percy is right. There has been an advance; but it is an advance within a return. He returns not only to his own work but also to the tradition of letters in America. Reflecting on the work of Herman Melville, Percy once gave passing praise to the structuralists' concept of intertextuality. *Moby Dick*, Percy writes, "was not only dedicated to Hawthorne, it was written at him" (*Signposts*, 200). He goes on to point out the paradoxical way Melville characterized his experience after writing his masterpiece. At once Melville felt "broiled in hellfire" and "spotless as a lamb." Percy notes that the paradox might be understood by what Melville described as the "ineffable sociability" he felt: "Surely this is the key to the paradox—the ineffable sociability in writing. Intertextuality, if you please. As lonely as is the craft of writing, it is the most social of vocations."[29]

At whom did Percy write his works? With whom did he feel these ineffable sociabilities? The answer perhaps rests in the concept of repetition. Since his fiction is explorative in nature, Percy not only names something new for his reader but also writes constantly at himself; he *repeats* himself. He pushes the boundaries back while remaining within limitation. What he says of Melville's work is equally true of his own: "As the narrative unfolds, one becomes aware that in its very telling, something else is being told, a ghostly narrative of great import told by a ghostly self, perhaps one's own shadow self" (*Signposts*, 201). *The Second Coming* repeats the story of Will Barrett, but it also repeats the account of the blue-dollar hawk, however transformed. That account, in turn, repeats the constitution of the self in metaphor, which as repetition repeats the mystery of language and narrative.

29. For more on Percy and classic American Literature, see Elżbieta H. Oleksy, *Plight in Common: Hawthorne and Percy* (New York, 1993).

Coda:
Autobiography,
Repetition, and Percy

I am having the
uncomfortable feeling of
having at last been stuck in
my slot—as a "Christian
Existentialist." I hear
sighs of relief all over: now
that they know what I am,
they don't have to worry
about me.

—Walker Percy to Shelby
Foote, January 29, 1979

Speaking at a memorial service in honor of
Walker Percy at Saint Ignatius Church in
New York City, Robert Giroux commented:
"We come here today to honor the memory
and the work of Walker Percy, a superb novelist, a distinguished man of letters, a witty
and searching critic, a great American. If I resist the adjective Southern, I am only following Dr. Percy's example."[1] Toward the end of
his eulogy, however, Giroux dramatically
sums up Percy's life and work with two
words that seem to emphasize the southern-
ness he earlier resisted: "[Percy] was truly a
man for all seasons, whose life and work ex-
emplified that pair of concepts all too rare today—probity and honor." Despite the fact

1. Robert Giroux *et al.*, *Walker Percy: 1916–1990*
(New York, 1991). There are no page numbers in this
booklet. Besides Giroux, other speakers included Shelby
Foote, Stanley Kauffmann, Patrick Samway, S.J., Mary
Lee Settle, Wilfrid Sheed, and Eudora Welty. I will make
further references to this booklet by citing the particular
speaker.

that the South has never been the sole proprietor of these virtues, Giroux nevertheless seems to link the two, the region and the qualities. He had earlier referred to Colonel John Pelham's appearance in Percy's witty "The Last Phil Donahue Show" in *Lost in the Cosmos*.[2] There Giroux characterizes Pelham as "a Confederate officer, representing probity and honor." Thus, while he refrains from the label in his opening remarks, he nevertheless seems to place Percy squarely in the South in his closing ones.

Giroux's wavering signals something students of Percy often encounter: the difficulty they have in placing him. This difficulty, furthermore, seems to be related to the category of repetition. If it is true that repetition as *inter esse* finds a prominent place in Percy's works, then it may not be surprising that Percy himself resisted labels. Labels foreclose possibility; they demand an adherence, one might say, to a prescribed proscription. That is, they place the abstract before the concrete. They make of the self a neat, rounded-off package. Percy not only resisted the label "southern," he also resisted "professional," "philosopher," and "linguistician." He did so, moreover, despite his having spent almost forty years of his life thinking and writing about the unique phenomenon of language.

In Chapter 2 I suggested that such a resistance might indicate what I called Percy's methodology of repetition. Not only did Percy return time and again to his "extraliterary" pursuit, but the posture of the nonprofessional, "being between," allowed him a fresh view of what "professional specializations" can too often foreclose in jargon and theoretical apparatus. Percy thus took the posture of the genuine researcher, not the technician. As he writes in "The Loss of the Creature": "The technician . . . [is] always offended by the genuine research man because the latter is usually a little vague and always humble before the thing; he doesn't have much use for the equipment or the jargon. Whereas the technician is never vague and never humble before the thing; he holds the thing disposed of by the principle, the formula, the textbook outline, and he thinks a great deal of equipment and jargon" (*MB,* 61). Such a researcher is not entirely different from Binx Bolling, who, although not as disposed to the "pure research" of science as his Aunt Emily seems to think, nevertheless goes out into the world and "doesn't miss a trick." Such a researcher is, in short, a *homo viator.*

2. In his talk Giroux mistakenly calls him "Palmer."

"Research" itself derives from the Middle French *recercher*, which means "to travel through, survey." Both words thus indicate a posture of wandering or wayfaring. As I tried to show in Chapters 1 and 2, *homo viator* is a label that both limits and opens possibility. The same could be said for research. As an exploration its posture is similar to that of *homo viator*—*i.e.,* it places one "no place." When all is said and done, there is always more to be said and done. There will always be those who go back to retrieve the inherited possibilities of the researcher's work. One's place never really solidifies; one is always displaced. Like *homo viator,* then, research is a label that resists labeling.

Despite his status as a researcher, Percy nevertheless used his own sort of tools, notably essays and novels. And the "thing" he explores in both his fiction and nonfiction is really "no-thing"—*i.e.,* the self that places itself in the world in and through language. Without the breakthrough into language, Percy argues, the self has no world. Already the sort of reflexivity I mentioned in the last chapter reveals itself. For Percy uses language to get at the self that is always and already immeshed in a world of language. The medium that is his tool is also the medium whose relation to the self and world he explores. Because the self and language are inextricably joined, one can step back from neither.

Yet because of language the self develops a self-consciousness. And what it experiences is a sense of its own displacement in language. The self cannot place it*self* as it places other things, and so it wanders, in search of a place that would quell the anxiety of its fundamental displacement. Percy's writing bears the indelible imprint of a self-consciously wandering self. It speaks of his own self and life, however transformed either may be in the final product. In his writing, as I suggest at the end of the last chapter, Percy *repeats himself.* Even an ostensibly "scientific" essay such as "Metaphor as Mistake" traces the attenuated links of a self who is both different and same—the "I" of the present writer and "the boy" around whose experience the writer frames part of his argument.

Repetition thus becomes necessary. Percy tries time and again in both the novels and the essays to come at his displacement in a new way. In a Faulkneresque comment to Linda Whitney Hobson, Percy said that his work up to that point (1981) had been a failure: "I think I've failed in these five novels and in *The Message in the Bottle,* but I've got a good idea for the next one. You know, I'll tell you a secret: I think the only thing that keeps the novelist going (and I'm sure that any other novelist would admit this) is that you are going to do the really big one" (*Con,* 225). Unlike Faulkner, Percy does not say that his works are "splendid failures." Rather, the impression he creates is that he forgets his previous failures to go after the "big one." Whether Percy ever wrote the big one is not for me to say. Readers must decide for themselves. But the phrase intrigues me. If it is taken not solely as a compound noun—*i.e.,* the masterwork—but as a noun modified by an adjective—*i.e.,* the big "one"—then Percy's comment suggests a search for the unity of repetition, which, again, is always tentative and attenuated.

This "one" Percy mentions sounds similar to the IT of the romantic, yet they nevertheless differ, I believe, in fundamental ways. Whereas the romantic's IT exists in a world of its own, cut off from lived time—the romantic sets "just beyond his reach the very thing he prizes" (*MG,* 215)—the "one" of repetition provides "hints and guesses" in lived time of what awaits in the fullness of time. Herein resides Percy's profound hope. The romantic cannot help but be disappointed because in recollection the IT has already been, and no experience can match it. The "one" Percy seeks, however, not only has been but also approaches from the future. It awaits actualization, as Kierkegaard suggests. Hence, Percy derives the impetus for his work in the hope that his resoluteness will provide, not the loss of recollection, but the gain and the unity of repetition: "I am myself again!" the poet of *Repetition* exclaims.

In this regard his works begin with himself as a denizen of the postmodern world who experiences himself as displaced in language, and they return to himself as somehow unified, however tentatively—else why continue to go after the big one?—in the difference of writing. In his writing Percy repeats his life and his self in the hope of creating the unity of self, life, and writing, which is autobiography. But just as *autos, bios,* and *graphein* are different elements of one word, so the self, life, and writing of Percy do not find a simple unity. Percy once wrote Foote: "Life is much stranger than art—and often more geometrical—My life breaks exactly in half: 1st half = growing up Southern and medical; 2nd half = imposing art on first half—3rd half? Sitting on bayou and repeating over and over again like old Buddenbrooks: *Kurios!*"[3] The sort of unity Percy attains finds apt expression in the "3rd half" of life. Such a displaced half suggests the openness of the autobiographical act, for once life has been transformed into art there is yet more life to live. Percy, like the eponymous hero of Thomas Mann's novel, can but sit, like Binx, lost in the mystery and curiosity of his existence at this place and time. The self and the life, then, are both different from and the same as the writing that portrays them. Yet, as I suggested in the last chapter, they find a reconciliation in the difference of metaphor. Percy's works begin and end as "autobiography," which, like "novel," is also a label that resists labeling.

Using the works of three critics in James Olney's collection, *Autobiography: Essays Theoretical and Critical,* Joseph Fichtelberg categorizes three approaches to the problem of the relation between self, life, and writing: "Olney's unity, Renza's difference, and Sprinker's multiplicity are the three possible responses to the problem of the subject in autobiography."[4] Does the self find unity in the telling of its story? Does it forever differ from the story told? Or does it endlessly multiply itself (and eventually evaporate) in the telling? I have tried to show that in reading autobiography as repetition in Percy's works *Yes* seems to be the answer to all three. I do not mean to be overly paradoxical here. What I suggest is that my reading of Percy's works and autobiography in light of each other has been an attempt to destruct the necessity of seeing autobiography as falling within the exclusive limits of one or the other school. All three "trouble with," as Olney puts it, "the self and consciousness and knowledge of it."[5] And Percy's works demonstrate a lifelong troubling with these same issues.

His research brought him face to face with the predicament of the postmodern attitude, and although I have read his works in a postmodern light, Percy himself often belittled the "postmodern project," especially the efforts by some of its proponents to deny any existence of the self. In a footnote

3. Walker Percy to Shelby Foote, September 14, 1972, in Percy Papers, SHC.

4. See Olney, "Some Versions," in *Autobiography: Essays,* ed. Olney, 236–67; Louis Renza, "The Veto of the Imagination: A Theory of Autobiography," 268–95; and Michael Sprinker's "Fictions of the Self: The End of Autobiography," 321–42. Joseph Fichtelberg, *The Complex Image: Faith and Method in American Autobiography* (Philadelphia, 1989), 4.

5. Olney, "Autobiography and the Cultural Moment," in *Autobiography: Essays,* ed. Olney, 23.

to the Intermezzo section of *Lost in the Cosmos,* Percy described deconstruction as the "whimsical stepchild" of the structuralism of Claude Lévi-Strauss and others (*LC,* 87). What seemed to have interested Percy about the postmodern era is not the casting off of the centuries-old shackles of Western tradition—especially the idea of the "self"—but the possibility of renovating that tradition, of retrieving something from it and rendering it again strange to his own age. Percy's unique postmodern project is the destructive one that Spanos, following Kierkegaard and Heidegger, sets forth. In his works Percy seeks new possibilities in the wake of the death of the modern age. He seems poignantly aware that his time is an age of "being between" the modern world and an age that, because it has no other name, has been called "postmodern." Percy's project does not destroy the self; rather, it de-structures the contemporary understanding of the self—as an organism with needs to be met, as a Jeffersonian Democrat, as a "California Guru," as an orbiting scientist—only to retrieve an inherited potentiality that "has been" in the tradition all along. He undertook such a project not in the hope of making that tradition "relevant" to this age, but in the hope of finding a name for the peculiar predicament we find ourselves in, immersed as we are in questions of self, language, and consciousness. Thus, his transformation of experience into art calls forth at once all three views of the relation between self, life, and writing. Percy's place remains elusive. In the errant label that autobiography provides, he seeks a place for the self whose only place is provided by the traveling of research. His research returns him—and the reader—to the strange label *homo viator.*

In her talk at the memorial service in New York City, Eudora Welty spoke about Percy's novels as an exercise in defamiliarization: "On first reading a novel by Walker Percy, we might rather soon ask ourselves, Where are we? Where in the world is he taking us? . . . What was until a moment ago a familiar time and place (even, perhaps, 'Southern') is signalling 'Danger!' . . . Where is Walker Percy taking us? We are still at home. But home lies before us in a different light, and its face is turned toward a new perspective, but it's still where we live. Only *we* may have altered."[6] Percy takes us somewhere that is ostensibly familiar yet really strange. In so doing he ends his exploration in the place it began. He returns us to our-

6. Eudora Welty, in *Walker Percy: 1916–1990,* ed. Giroux *et al.*

selves so that we know ourselves to be both at home and not at home, at the place of exploration, the no place of the self whose life is a wandering in the strangeness of language and writing. The unity of Percy's self, life, and writing derives from the strange unity of repetition and the limited possibility of autobiography.

Bibliography

Allen, William Rodney. *Walker Percy: A Southern Wayfarer.* Jackson, 1986.

Altieri, Charles. "How Critics Contribute to Postmodernism: Some Thoughts on the Positions of Gerald Graff and William Spanos." *Par Rapport,* XI (Summer, 1979), 123–35.

Auden, W. H. "Knight of Doleful Countenance." *The New Yorker,* May 25, 1968, pp. 141–42, 146–48, 151–54, 157–58.

Augustine, Saint. *The Confessions of St. Augustine.* Translated by Rex Warner. New York, 1963.

Benveniste, Emile. *Problems in General Linguistics.* Coral Gables, Fla., 1973.

Bigelow, Pat. *Kierkegaard and the Problem of Writing.* Tallahassee, 1987.

Bigger, Charles P. "Walker Percy and the Resonance of the Word." *Southern Quarterly,* XVIII (1980), 43–54.

Binding, Karl, and Alfred Hoche. *The Release of the Destruction of Life Devoid of Value.* Leipzig, 1920.

Bloom, Harold. *The American Religion: The Emergence of the Post-Christian Nation.* New York, 1992.

Bosworth, Sheila. "Women in the Fiction of Walker Percy." Paper delivered at the 1993 Walker Percy Symposium, March 20, 1993, Covington, La., sponsored by the St. Tammany Parish Library.

Bové, Paul A. "Cleanth Brooks and Modern Irony: A Kierkegaardian Critique." *boundary 2,* IV (1976), 727–59.

Broudy, H. S. "Kierkegaard's Doctrine of Indirect Communication." *Journal of Philosophy,* LVIII (1961), 225–33.

Broughton, Panthea Reid. "Walker Percy and the Myth of the Innocent Eye." In *Literary Romanticism in America,* edited by William L. Andrews. Baton Rouge, 1981.

———, ed. *The Art of Walker Percy: Stratagems for Being.* Baton Rouge, 1979.

Ciuba, Gary M. *Walker Percy: Books of Revelations.* Athens, 1991.

Cole, J. Preston. *The Problematic Self in Kierkegaard and Freud*. New Haven, 1971.

Coles, Robert. *Walker Percy: An American Search*. Boston, 1978.

Cox, James M. *Recovering Literature's Lost Ground: Essays in American Autobiography*. Baton Rouge, 1989.

Crites, Stephen. "The Author and the Authorship: Recent Kierkegaard Literature." *Journal of the American Academy of Religion*, XXXVIII (1970), 37–54.

———. *In the Twilight of Christendom*. Chambersburg, Pa., 1972.

———. "The Narrative Quality of Experience." *Journal of the American Academy of Religion*, XXXIV (September, 1971), 291–311. Reprinted in *Why Narrative? Readings in Narrative Theology*, edited by Stanley Hauerwas and L. Gregory Jones. Grand Rapids, Mich., 1989.

———. "Pseudonymous Authorship as Art and as Act." In *Kierkegaard: A Collection of Critical Essays*, edited by Josiah Thompson. Garden City, N.Y., 1972.

Culler, Jonathan. "Man the Symbol-Monger." Review of *The Message in the Bottle*, by Walker Percy. *Yale Review*, LXV (1976), 261–66.

Dickey, James. Review of *The Last Gentleman*, by Walker Percy. *American Scholar*, XXXVII (1968), 524.

Durfee, Harold A. "The Second Stage of Kierkegaardian Scholarship in America." *International Philosophical Quarterly*, III (1963), 121–39.

Eakin, Paul John. *Fictions in Autobiography: Studies in the Art of Self-Invention*. Princeton, 1985.

Edelman, Gerald M. *Bright Air, Brilliant Fire: On the Matter of the Mind*. New York, 1992.

Eliade, Mircea. *Cosmos and History: The Myth of the Eternal Return*. Translated by Willard Trask. Bollingen Series, XLVI. Princeton, 1971.

Eliot, T. S. *The Complete Poems and Plays: 1909–1950*. New York, 1971.

Fichtelberg, Joseph. *The Complex Image: Faith and Method in American Autobiography*. Philadelphia, 1989.

Foote, Shelby. Papers, #4038. Southern Historical Collection, Library of the University of North Carolina, Chapel Hill.

Frank, Joseph. "Spatial Form in Modern Literature." *Sewanee Review*, LIII (1945), 221–40, 432–56, 643–53.

Fraser, Ronald. *In Search of a Past: The Manor House, Amnersfield, 1933–1945*. London, 1984.

Freud, Sigmund. *Dora: An Analysis of a Case of Hysteria*. New York, 1963.

Giroux, Robert, *et al. Walker Percy: 1916–1990*. New York, 1991.

Gonzalez, Justo L. *A History of Christian Thought*. Vol. I of 3 vols. Nashville, 1970.

Gray, Richard. *Writing the South: Ideas of an American Region*. Cambridge, Eng., 1986.

Griffith, Richard M. "Repetition: Constantin (S.) Constantius." *Journal of Existential Psychiatry,* II (1962), 437–48.

Guardini, Romano. *The End of the Modern World: A Search for Orientation.* Translated by Joseph Theman and Herbert Burke. New York, 1956.

Gunn, Janet Varner. *Autobiography: Toward a Poetics of Experience.* Philadelphia, 1982.

Habermas, Jurgen. "Modernity Versus Postmodernity." *New German Critique,* XXII (Winter, 1981), 3–14.

Harbage, Alfred, ed. *William Shakespeare: The Complete Works.* New York, 1969.

Hardy, John Edward. *The Fiction of Walker Percy.* Urbana, 1987.

———. "Percy and Place: Some Beginnings and Endings." *Southern Quarterly,* XVIII (1980), 5–25.

Hartman, Robert S. "The Self in Kierkegaard." *Journal of Existential Psychiatry,* II (1962), 409–36.

Hauerwas, Stanley and L. Gregory Jones, eds. *Why Narrative? Readings in Narrative Theology.* Grand Rapids, Mich., 1989.

Heidegger, Martin. *Being and Time.* Translated by John Macquarrie and Edward Robinson. New York, 1962.

Heinemann, F. H. "Origin and Repetition." *Review of Metaphysics,* IV (1950–51), 201–14.

Held, Matthew. "The Historical Kierkegaard: Faith or Gnosis." *Journal of Religion,* XXXVII (1957), 260–66.

Hobson, Fred. *The Southern Writer in the Postmodern World.* Athens, 1991.

Hobson, Linda Whitney. *Understanding Walker Percy.* Columbia, S.C., 1988.

———. *Walker Percy: A Comprehensive Descriptive Bibliography.* New Orleans, 1988.

———. " 'Watching, Listening and Waiting': The Mode of the Seeker in Walker Percy's Fiction." *Southern Literary Journal,* XX (1988), 43–50.

Howland, Mary Deems. *The Gift of the Other: Gabriel Marcel's Concept of Intersubjectivity in Walker Percy's Novels.* Pittsburgh, 1990.

Humphries, Josephine. *Dreams of Sleep.* New York, 1984.

Johann, Fr. Robert, S.J. "Charity and Time." *Cross Currents,* IX (1959), 140–49.

Jonas, Hans. *The Gnostic Religion.* Boston, 1958.

Keller, Helen. *The Story of My Life.* New York, 1954.

Kennedy, J. Gerald. "The Semiotics of Memory: Suicide in *The Second Coming.*" *Delta* (Montpellier, France), XIII (1981), 103–25.

Kierkegaard, Søren. *Concluding Unscientific Postscript.* Translated by David F. Swenson and Walter Lowrie. Princeton, 1941.

———. *Either/Or.* Edited and translated by Howard V. Hong and Edna H. Hong. 2 vols. Princeton, 1987.

————. *Fear and Trembling/Repetition.* Edited and translated by Howard V. Hong and Edna H. Hong. Princeton, 1983.

————. *The Present Age.* Translated by Alexander Dru. New York, 1962.

————. *The Sickness unto Death.* Edited and translated by Howard V. Hong and Edna H. Hong. Princeton, 1980.

Kisor, Henry. *What's That Pig Outdoors? A Memoir of Deafness.* New York, 1990.

Lang, Berel. *Act and Idea in the Nazi Genocide.* Chicago, 1990.

————, ed. *Writing and the Holocaust.* New York, 1988.

Lasch, Christopher. "Probing Gnosticism and Its Modern Derivatives." *New Oxford Review,* LVII (December, 1990), 6–9.

Lawry, Edward G. "Literature as Philosophy." *The Monist,* LXIII (1980), 547–57.

Lawson, Lewis A. "The Cross and the Delta: Walker Percy's Anthropology." In *Walker Percy: Novelist and Philosopher,* edited by Jan Nordby Gretlund and Karl-Heinz Westarp. Jackson, 1991.

————. *Following Percy: Essays on Walker Percy's Work.* Troy, N.Y., 1988.

————. "Hardy Thinking on Percy." Review of *The Fiction of Walker Percy,* by John Edward Hardy. *Southern Literary Journal,* XXI (1989), 113–18.

————. "Walker Percy." In *The History of Southern Literature,* edited by Louis D. Rubin, Jr., *et al.* Baton Rouge, 1985.

————. "Will Barrett Under the Telescope." *Southern Literary Journal,* XX (1988), 16–41.

Lawson, Lewis A., and Victor A. Kramer, eds. *Conversations with Walker Percy.* Jackson, 1985.

————. *More Conversations with Walker Percy.* Jackson, 1993.

Levi, Primo. *The Drowned and the Saved.* Translated by Raymond Rosenthal. New York, 1988 (first Italian publication, 1986).

————. *Moments of Reprieve.* Translated by Ruth Feldman. New York, 1987 (first Italian publication, 1981).

————. *The Periodic Table.* Translated by Raymond Rosenthal. New York, 1984 (first Italian publication, 1975).

————. *The Reawakening.* Translated by Stuart Woolf. New York, 1987 (first Italian publication, 1963).

————. *The Sixth Day and Other Tales.* Translated by Raymond Rosenthal. New York, 1990 (first Italian publication, 1966, 1977).

————. *Survival in Auschwitz.* Translated by Stuart Woolf. New York, 1961 (first Italian publication, 1958).

Lukács, Georg. *The Theory of the Novel.* Cambridge, Mass., 1971.

Luschei, Martin. *The Sovereign Wayfarer: Walker Percy's Diagnosis of the Malaise.* Baton Rouge, 1972.

Marcel, Gabriel. *The Philosophy of Existentialism.* New York, 1956.

McCarthy, Mary. *Memories of a Catholic Girlhood.* New York, 1957.

McCombs, Phil. "Century of Thanatos: Walker Percy and His 'Subversive Message.'" *Southern Review,* n.s., XXIV (1988), 808–24.

McKeon, Michael. *The Origins of the English Novel, 1600–1740.* Baltimore, 1987.

McLane, Henry Earl, Jr. "Kierkegaard's Use of the Category of Repetition: An Attempt to Discern the Structure and Unity of His Thought." Ph.D. dissertation, Yale University, 1961.

Megill, Allan. "What does the Term 'Postmodern' Mean?" *Annals of Scholarship,* VI (1989), 129–51.

Miller, J. Hillis. *Fiction and Repetition.* Cambridge, Mass., 1982.

Minear, Paul S. "Thanksgiving as a Synthesis of the Temporal and Eternal." *Anglican Theological Review,* XXXVIII (1956), 4–14.

———. "The Time of Hope in the New Testament." *Scottish Journal of Theology,* VI (1953), 337–61.

Muilenburg, James. "The Biblical View of Time." *Harvard Theological Review,* LIV (1961), 221–52.

Murphy, Christina. "'Exalted in This Romantic Place': Narrative Voice and the Structure of Walker Percy's *The Moviegoer.*" *Publications of the Mississippi Philological Association* (1984), 55–68.

Oleksy, Elżbieta H. *Plight in Common: Hawthorne and Percy.* New York, 1993.

Olney, James., ed. *Autobiography: Essays Theoretical and Critical.* Princeton, 1980.

———. "'I Was Born': Slave Narratives, Their Status as Autobiography and as Literature." In *The Slave's Narrative,* edited by Charles Davis and Henry Louis Gates. Oxford, Eng., 1985.

———. *Metaphors of Self: The Meaning of Autobiography.* Princeton, 1972.

Percy, Walker. "Carnival in Gentilly." University of Houston *Forum,* III (1960), 4–18.

———. *Lancelot.* New York, 1977.

———. *The Last Gentleman.* New York, 1966.

———. *Lost in the Cosmos.* New York, 1983.

———. *Love in the Ruins.* New York, 1971.

———. *The Message in the Bottle.* New York, 1975.

———. *The Moviegoer.* New York, 1961.

———. Papers, #4294. Southern Historical Collection, Library of the University of North Carolina, Chapel Hill.

———. *The Second Coming.* New York, 1980.

———. *Signposts in a Strange Land.* Edited by Patrick Samway, S.J. New York, 1991.

————. *The Thanatos Syndrome.* New York, 1987.

————. "Why Are You a Catholic?: The Late Novelist's Parting Reflections." *Crisis,* (September, 1990), 14–19. Reprinted in *Living Philosophies: The Reflections of Some Eminent Men and Women of Our Time,* edited by Clifton Fadiman. New York, 1990.

Percy, William Alexander. *Lanterns on the Levee.* With an Introduction by Walker Percy. Baton Rouge, 1973.

Perl, Jeffrey M. *The Tradition of the Return.* Princeton, 1984.

Pickering, Samuel F., Jr. *The Right Distance.* Athens, 1987.

Pindell, Richard. "Basking in the Eye of the Storm: The Esthetics of Loss in Walker Percy's *The Moviegoer.*" *boundary 2,* IV (1975), 219–30.

Poteat, Patricia Lewis. *Walker Percy and the Old Modern Age: Reflections on Language, Argument and the Telling of Stories.* Baton Rouge, 1985.

Puech, Henri-Charles. "Gnosis and Time." In *Man and Time,* edited by Joseph Campbell. New York, 1957.

Quagliano, Anthony. "Existential Modes in *The Moviegoer.*" Washington State University *Research Studies,* XLV (1977), 214–23.

Reed, Walter. *An Exemplary History of the Novel.* Chicago, 1981.

Ricoeur, Paul. *Interpretation Theory: Discourse and the Surplus of Meaning.* Fort Worth, 1976.

————. "Narrative Time." *Critical Inquiry,* VII (1980), 169–90.

————. *Time and Narrative.* 3 vols. Chicago, 1984, 1986, 1988.

Rubin, Louis D., Jr. "The Boll Weevil, the Iron Horse, and the End of the Line." In *A Gallery of Southerners,* by Louis D. Rubin, Jr. Baton Rouge, 1982.

————. "Walker Percy: 1916–1990." *Southern Literary Journal,* XXIII (1990), 5–7.

Said, Edward W. "On Repetition." In *The Literature of Fact,* edited by Angus Fletcher. New York, 1976.

Samway, Patrick, S.J. "Gaps and Codes: Walker Percy's 'Carnival in Gentilly.' " *Shenandoah,* XLIII (Spring, 1993), 47–56.

————. "An Interview with Walker Percy." *America,* February 15, 1986, p. 122.

————. "A Writer at Home in Louisiana." In *Cross, Crosier, and Crucible: A Volume Celebrating the Bicentennial of a Catholic Diocese in Louisiana (1793–1993),* edited by Glenn R. Conrad. Lafayette, La., 1993.

Schleifer, Ronald, and Robert Markley, eds. *Kierkegaard and Literature: Irony, Repetition, and Criticism.* Norman, Okla., 1984.

Schrag, Calvin O. "Kierkegaard's Existential Reflections on Time." *The Personalist,* XLII (1961), 149–61.

Scott, Nathan A., Jr. *The Broken Center: Studies in the Theological Horizon of Modern Literature.* New Haven, 1966.

Simpson, Lewis P. *The Brazen Face of History: Studies in the Literary Consciousness in America.* Baton Rouge, 1980.

———. *The Dispossessed Garden.* Athens, 1975.

———. "Walker Percy's Vision of the Modern World." The Flora Levy Lecture in the Humanities, March 7, 1991, University of Southwestern Louisiana.

Spanos, William V. "The Critical Imperatives of Alienation: The Theological Perspective of Nathan Scott's Literary Criticism." *Journal of Religion,* XLVIII (January, 1968), 89–103.

———. "Heidegger, Kierkegaard, and the Hermeneutic Circle: Toward a Postmodern Theory of Interpretation as Disclosure." *boundary 2,* IV (1976), 455–88.

———. "The Indifference of *Différance:* Retrieving Heidegger's De-struction." *Annals of Scholarship,* II (1981), 109–29.

———. "Modern Drama and the Aristotelian Tradition: The Formal Imperatives of Absurd Time." *Contemporary Literature,* XII (1971), 345–73.

———. "Modern Literary Criticism and the Spatialization of Time." *Journal of Aesthetics and Art Criticism,* XXIX (1970), 87–104.

———. *Repetitions: The Postmodern Occasion in Literature and Culture.* Baton Rouge, 1987.

———. " 'Wanna Go Home, Baby?': *Sweeney Agonistes* as Drama of the Absurd." *PMLA,* LXXXV (1968), 8–20.

Spivey, Ted R. *The Writer as Shaman: The Pilgrimages of Conrad Aiken and Walker Percy.* Macon, Ga., 1986.

Stack, George J. "Kierkegaard and the Phenomenology of Repetition." *Journal of Existentialism,* VII (1966–67), 111–28.

———. "Repetition in Kierkegaard and Freud." *The Personalist,* LVIII (1977), 249–60.

Stevenson, John W. "Walker Percy: The Novelist as Poet." *Southern Review, n.s.,* XVII (1981), 164–74.

Taylor, Jerome. *In Search of Self: Life, Death and Walker Percy.* Cambridge, Mass., 1986.

———. *Walker Percy's Heroes: A Kierkegaardian Analysis.* New York, 1983.

Tellote, J. P. "Charles Peirce and Walker Percy: From Semiotic to Narrative." *Southern Quarterly,* XVIII (1980), 65–79.

Thomas, J. Heywood. "Kierkegaard and Existentialism." *Scottish Journal of Theology,* VI (1953), 379–95.

Tolson, Jay. *Pilgrim in the Ruins: A Life of Walker Percy.* New York, 1992.

Voegelin, Eric. *The New Science of Politics.* Chicago, 1952.

———. *Science, Politics and Gnosticism.* Chicago, 1968.

Watt, Ian. *The Rise of the Novel*. Berkeley, 1957.

Wertham, Frederic. *A Sign for Cain: An Exploration of Human Violence*. New York, 1966.

Widenmann, Robert. "Some Aspects of Time in Aristotle and Kierkegaard." *Kierkegaardiana* 7, Copenhagen, 1971.

Wood, Ralph C. *The Comedy of Redemption: Christian Faith and Comic Vision in Five American Novelists*. Notre Dame, 1988.

Wyatt-Brown, Bertram. *The House of Percy: Honor, Melancholy, and Imagination in a Southern Family*. New York, 1994.

Zamora, Lois Parkinson. "Apocalypse and Renewal: Walker Percy and the U.S. South." In *Writing the Apocalypse: Historical Vision in Contemporary U.S. and Latin American Fiction*, by Lois Parkinson Zamora. Cambridge, Mass., 1989.

Index

Abraham, 32, 35–36

Abstracted posture, 50

Abstraction, 60, 61

Adams, Henry, 134

Aesthetics: aesthetic apprehension, 6, 18, 32; based on language, 18; aesthetic sphere, 25, 34, 63, 68, 101; the aesthetic, 26, 32, 33, 63, 73, 123; aesthetic activity, 28; aesthetic strategy, 29, 32; aesthetic category, 68, 93; aesthetic repetition, 68, 69; aesthetic age, 112

Aeterno modo, 31, 37, 49

Alienation, 82, 83, 84

Allen, William Rodney, 3, 4, 26, 81, 113, 134

Americans, 99, 105

Angelic infinite, 31

Angelic knowledge, 117

Angelism/bestialism, 60, 82, 92, 109, 110, 111. *See also* Bestialism

Angels, 10, 109, 111, 139

Antaeus, 17, 35

Apocalypse, 90, 104, 112, 119

Aquinas, Thomas, 103

Aristotle, 24, 128

Art: 152, 153; transcendence of, 58, 59, 64; as sign, 61, 62; as salvific, 63; as naming, 125. *See also* Experience

Artist, 59

Atemporality, 96, 97, 104, 114, 119

Augustine, St., 6, 37, 116, 139, 143

Autobiography: as movement, 3, 123; as

study of consciousness, 3; theory of, 4, 14; definition of, 5, 13, 14, 15; as self-reflexive, 6, 7, 9; as history, 13, 14; as transforming experience into art, 15; as repetition, 35, 43

Autos, 4, 47, 64, 124, 135, 152

Barrett, Mr. Ed, 87

Barrett, Will: in *The Last Gentleman,* 73, 74, 76, 78, 80–85, 105; in *The Second Coming,* 106, 113, 139–41, 143–47; mentioned, xi, 2, 60

Barth, John, 136

Beast, 10, 31, 111, 139

Beethoven, 58

Being-between. See *Inter esse*

Bestialism, 109, 114, 117, 124. *See also* Angelism/bestialism

Bigger, Charles, 125, 127, 128

Binding, Karl, 115

Bios: 4, 124, 135, 152; as historical course of life, 22; as vital principle, 22

Bloom, Harold, 95, 97–100, 102

Bolling, Binx: 68, 73, 76, 91, 108, 138; as consumer, 64, 66; compared to Quentin Compson, 64; as scientist, 65, 67; as narrator, 66; as romantic, 69; mentioned, 2, 60, 105, 131, 150

Boomer, Fr., 87

Bosworth, Sheila, 60

Bové, Paul, 6, 19, 72